ESTHER

God in Control, But Concealed

Albert McShane

JOHN RITCHIE LTD.
40 BEANSBURN, KILMARNOCK, SCOTLAND

ISBN O 946351 48 1

Cover Picture: The cliffside tomb of the Persian King Ahasuerus
selected from *The New Illustrated Bible Dictionary*,
published Thomas Nelson inc. Nashville.

Typeset by: EM-DEE Productions, Glasgow
Printed by: Bell and Bain Ltd., Glasgow

Contents

ESTHER AND THE DECREE

THE KING'S DECREE ON BEHALF OF THE JEWS

The Book of Esther

INTRODUCTION

For many centuries there had been little in the lands of the Middle East to excite the interest of the rest of the world; but when the war between Iran and Iraq erupted, and more recently the short but sharp war in Kuwait, then these focused attention on that part of the world, and aroused rulers to see the powers that were centred in the area. The ancient name of Iran was Persia, and it is important to note that there is an entire book in the OT devoted to events centred in one of its capital cities, Shushan. That book is Esther, and in its chapters we are granted an insight into the heart of Persian life some two and one half millennia ago, howbeit, an insight spanning only a brief space of time. The events recorded in this short book cover a period of approximately five years, so the light it gives us is like a flash of lightning, which appears suddenly, and disappears just as quickly. Even so, it is well to value this inspired record of the affairs in what was then the world's greatest empire, and to learn if we can the lessons it has for us in our time. While reading it we have to bear in mind that, had it not been that a crisis arose in the experience of the Jews in captivity, this story would never have been given a place in Holy Scripture.

There is possibly no other book in the OT which has attracted so little attention amongst expositors as the Book of Esther, for, apart from writers whose commentaries cover the entire OT and of necessity must deal with it, very few of them have been drawn to its pages as a field of special study. This is not surprising, for it is the most secular of all the writings of the OT. Those who are interested in the great theological subjects of the Scriptures, such as *deity, prophecy, eschatology* or *ecclesiology* will search its pages in vain for any help. It is not quoted in the NT; throughout its chapters the name of the Lord does not appear, nor is the ritual of sacrifice mentioned; even on the occasions when we would expect prayer to be made it is notably absent, and, what is even more strange, when great deliverances were experienced there is not one outburst of thanksgiving. There are reasons for these omissions which will be looked at later.

The question might well be asked, "Why was such a book given a place in the canon of Scripture?" Surprisingly enough, it was not only included in the sacred writings, but there is no record of any serious controversy over its inclusion. Those who first possessed it were satisfied as to its inspiration, and were happy to position it amongst the historical books. The two post-captivity books which precede it, Ezra and Nehemiah, show how the Lord wrought for the good of the returned captives even in the midst of opposition, but in Esther we are shown how the Lord wrought for the good of His people who remained in captivity. In His working, however, He keeps out of sight, and His help is not recognised nor publicly owned by them.

We must realise that though in our Bibles it is placed after Nehemiah, what is recorded in it took place much earlier. Most have noticed that between ch. 6 and ch. 7 of Ezra there is a considerable lapse of time extending to about sixty years; it was some time about the middle of this period that the events of Esther occurred. Therefore the Jews who took advantage of the decree of Cyrus had left the land of their captivity some eighty years before Ezra came up to instruct them. If this be so, he was still amongst the captives during the time of Esther and may well have been acquainted with the great crisis at Shushan.

THE WRITER

Much speculation surrounds the question of who wrote the book. Some have thought that Mordecai was the penman, others that Ezra wrote it, but we have no proof as to who was the human instrument employed. Of this we are sure: whoever he was, he had access to the archives of the Persian empire. No less than four times we are told that what occurred was recorded and placed in this official depository (2:23; 6:1; 9:32; 10:2). There are at least two reasons why Mordecai was not the writer of the book. Firstly, had he written it he would have used the first person when referring to himself, and secondly, he would not have praised his own doings in the way that they are extolled. Those acquainted with the Hebrew language are satisfied that the style of *Ezra* is so different from that of *Esther* that it is clear *he* was not the one employed. However, two facts are obvious: one is that the writer had a full knowledge of the details of the events narrated in it, and the other is that he lived some time after they had occurred. Perhaps the best suggestion is that one of the chamberlains in charge of the king's treasury originally wrote it for the king, and deposited it in the royal archives. If this were so, it would explain why the religious element was entirely excluded from it. If the writer was a God-fearing Jew he could easily have kept a copy of the original, and preserved it for his own people, who were the special subjects involved in this part of Persian history.

THE TIME WHEN IT WAS WRITTEN

Before any date can be set for the compilation of the Book of Esther a major point must be settled. It is this: there are three kings in Scripture which bear the title "Ahasuerus"; to which of these does the author of Esther refer? The comment "this is Ahasuerus which reigned from India even unto Ethiopia" (1:1) is no doubt intended to identify the king in question. It could not be the one referred to in Dan 9:1, for the kingdom of Persia at the beginning of his reign was not so extensive as the hundred and twenty-seven provinces mentioned in Esther ch. 1; nor is it likely to be the one referred to in Ezra 4:6, for he had a full knowledge of the Jews, and had no need, in the twelfth year of his reign, to be informed by Haman of their existence. Most writers, therefore, conclude that the Ahasuerus of Esther is the son of Darius, and called by the Greeks, Xerxes. If this be the king, the date of the events can be decided fairly accurately, for he reigned from 486 BC - 465 BC. Obviously some time had passed before the record of the events narrated in the book was compiled, otherwise it would not have been needful to point out which Ahasuerus was on the throne when they occurred. We shall not be too far astray if we put the date of the book at around 450 BC.

SPECIAL FEATURES OF THE BOOK

Perhaps the most amazing feature of this strange book is its evidence of God working yet remaining in the shadows. Those who know Him and are acquainted with His doings have no doubt that He was overruling in all the events recorded. The lines we sing, "God moves in a mysterious way His wonders to perform", were never more applicable than they were in the happenings of the palace of Persia.

His hand can be seen in placing Esther in a position of influence; in delaying the day of destruction of the Jews for almost a year, so that their deliverance could be accomplished; in causing the king to order that the man who plotted to kill Mordecai, the Jew, be the one who must lead him through Shushan and publicly proclaim his worthiness of highest honour; in promoting the despised Jew to the post of prime minister.

It is obvious that nothing religious appears in this book: the reason for this is that it was written in such a way as not to cause any offence to the Persian beliefs. It was assumed by the writer that the Jews who would read it would have no problem in their minds as to who was working for them, so they could whisper to themselves and to one another, "This is the Lord's doing". However there are those who believe that while the name of the Lord is not mentioned, it does occur in a cryptic way at least four times in the book. The original Hebrew had no vowels, so the word Jehovah was represented by the four consonants J H V H. In ch. 5:4 there are four words following each other whose initial letters are these consonants in the proper order. In ch. 7:7 this is again to be seen. The same consonants are to be found, but in reverse order, in ch. 1:20 and in ch. 5:13. To a Persian the text would read as though nothing special was involved, but the mind of a Jew, who had the secret, would be turned to think of the Lord as he read these passages.

Already we have mentioned the fact that those religious exercises we expect to find amongst the people of God, even when they are away in heart from Him, are absent from Esther. They are not only omitted, but studiously avoided, for there is no reference in it to any one or any people calling upon God, neither is there any mention of false gods or the worship of idols. Doubtless the Persians had their objects of worship, and praised their gods when they were successful in war. We also know it was because the Jews had turned to idolatry that they had been transported to the land of idols, yet throughout the Book of Esther there is no mention of any such religious activity. The nearest to any belief in unseen powers was when Haman cast lots to discover the luckiest day to execute his wicked plan, but this was an exercise motivated by nothing more than mere superstition.

Another striking feature of the book is the attention the writer pays to details. Whether we read of the palace with its luxurious furnishings (ch. 1), or the purification of the maidens (ch. 2), or the trappings on Mordecai (ch. 6), or the overturning of the plot to destroy the Jews (ch. 8), every little item is mentioned.

We would have expected that a book like Esther, written in a strange land and having no religious element in it, would be studded with unique words, but this is not the case. Though there are some words of a Persian origin found in its pages, these are surprisingly few. This would imply that the scribe was a Jew who had not forgotten his native language, even though it was not commonly spoken in the land of his captivity.

Unlike Daniel, who was ever conscientious regarding the law of his God, the Jews in Esther, as far as the record goes, had no such scruples. We know why Mordecai did not bow the knee to Haman, and he knew why, but not a word of explanation for this is given in the book. Neither is there any mention of the problems Esther encountered in having to live amongst the heathen in the court of a despotic king. Similarly, they are unlike the prophet in that there is no reference to any desires for the land of their fathers, nor is there any hint of a longing for either Jerusalem or the temple (cf. Dan 9). All is worded so as to imply that the Jews felt at home in Persia, as long as they were allowed to carry on with their normal way of living.

Another feature of this book which may not be noticed at first reading is the rise and fall in the fortune of each of its characters. They are like ships on a stormy sea: no sooner exalted to the crest of the wave, than humiliated to the lowest depths. Whether we think of Ahasuerus at his pompous banquet humiliated by the refusal of his wife to obey his demand and show herself to the assembled lords; or of Vashti herself with her private banquet being divorced and despised; or of Mordecai now elated at the exaltation of his cousin to be queen, and now crying on the street like a child; or of Haman exalted to lofty heights by the king, and then made to escort around the city Mordecai, the man he most detested, and to announce to all that this was the man whom the king delighted to honour; or of the thrilled enemies of the Jews who thought they were going to have a heyday gathering up the spoils of the Jews, but instead were gathering up the dead bodies of their own loved ones; in each case exaltation ended in humiliation. However, it is good to see that the story does not end in the valley, but on the high note of Mordecai's exaltation.

LINKS WITH OTHER BOOKS

There are two books in the OT which bear the names of women, Ruth and Esther. In the former we are shown how God can bring a poor Gentile into relationship with His people; in the latter we are shown how He can exalt the Jew to the highest place of honour amongst the Gentiles. In both we learn that God works for His own, even when they are unworthy and disobedient, indeed, even when they are unconscious of His operations. Another book in the OT which has at least one feature in common with Esther is the Song of Songs, for there is no mention of the Lord in it either. Very few who read this love song are not aware that it illustrates in poetic language the relationship of the Lord to His people. Likewise most who read Esther conclude that it shows God's interest in His people, the Jews. Esther, being allocated as the closing book of the history of the nation, has in it some interesting links with Exodus, the book which tells of the beginning of its history. Both books have this in common, that the enemy's plan was to wipe out the people of God. Just as Pharaoh decreed that the sons of Israel were to be drowned, so Haman decreed that Mordecai was to be hanged and his people spoiled. However, God saw to it that Pharaoh and his army were drowned, and likewise that Haman and his sons were hanged; so both enemies reaped what they sowed. Again both enemies fell at the very time when they were all but sure that their evil intent would be executed. However there is a noted contrast between the two stories, for while the spoils of Egypt were taken from the Egyptians, we are told twice in Esther that the Jews laid not their hand on the spoils of their enemies. One other important link between these two books is that each of the great deliverances granted was celebrated by the keeping of a feast, so that annually Israel remembered two occasions when the Lord intervened and delivered them from their enemies, the one at the feast of Passover, the other at the feast of Purim.

Perhaps we can see in Esther certain links with the Book of Daniel, for just as he would not submit to the decree of the king and had to suffer for his stand, so Mordecai refused to bow the knee to Haman and exposed himself, as well as his people, to his wrath. The day came when Daniel was dressed in royal apparel and had a gold chain about his neck, and likewise the man Mordecai had the royal apparel put upon him and a crown put upon his head.

The two companion post-captivity books, Ezra and

Nehemiah, have also certain links with Esther. One feature common to all three is the amount of correspondence by letters which passed between the rulers and the people. Throughout the lands of Israel's captivity there appeared to be no scarcity of scribes to write letters, nor lack of couriers to deliver them. On occasions they brought sad news to the recipients, and at other times they brought news of relief. A second feature of these books is the opposition of the enemy manifestly shown toward the Jews, whether in the building of the House in Ezra, the building of the wall in Nehemiah, or the plot of Haman in Esther. A third feature of all three books is that all that they record is centred in great cities. In Esther, Shushan is the hub around which all the events revolve, and in Ezra and Nehemiah all the attention is focused on the city of Jerusalem.

However, what is most outstanding is not the similarity of Esther to these two books, but rather its contrast. All that we expected to find in Esther, but was absent from it, appears in abundance in the other two books. For example, the important matters of prayer, thanksgiving, the offering of sacrifices, and attention to God's law are all seen in them to be given their rightful place. In neither of the former books are we shown the inner workings of the court of the Persian king, whereas this is a striking feature of Esther. When we consider that only ten percent of the Jews returned to the land of their fathers, we would have expected to learn something of how the vast number fared in the land of their captivity, but Ezra and Nehemiah are silent about them; only in Esther do we learn anything of their experiences.

One more book has some links with Esther; it is Job. At the introduction of Job we are told of the great feast that his sons had in one of their estates, and Esther begins likewise with a great feast. The wealth of Job himself is given in detail, as is the wealth and pomp of Ahasuerus. The sad sight of the patriarch sitting on ashes, corresponds with Mordecai standing weeping in the street of Shushan. The trial of Job brought out the true state of the men who were thought to be his friends, as did the trial of Mordecai and his people bring out the true state of those who surrounded them. If Job had seen the end of his experience it would have eased his sorrow immensely, and if Mordecai had seen the end of his trial, he could not have cried even had he attempted to do so.

THE PURPOSE OF IT

We might well ask why such a strange composition found its way into the Holy Scriptures. One vital lesson it teaches is that God is sovereign, and works out His purpose wherever He will, and that even when men are unconscious of His so doing. We are accustomed to reading of His disclosures to His servants the prophets, and of the many times He confided in men like them and told them what He was about to do, so that it was no surprise to them when these things occurred. This book gives a sample of something outside the pale of revelation, and teaches us that throughout the entire universe, even in the darkest corners of the earth, His hand is on the helm steering the ship of His counsels to its destined harbour.

Another purpose of the book is to demonstrate that even in the most adverse circumstances the Jew eventually prevails. This principle was exemplified as early in their history as Joseph; it was seen also in Moses. For though both were humiliated in Egypt, yet both rose high even in the estimation of the respective Pharaohs. Later the man Daniel, another captive, was elevated both by the Chaldean rulers, Nebuchadnezzar and Belshazzar, and later by the

Persian king, Darius. The kings of world empires were clearly taught that there was no holding down of God's representatives, for they were like a cork in water: they ever tended to float to the top.

A further lesson the book is meant to teach is the weakness of men in high places. Poor Ahasuerus imagined he had supreme power, that he was a despot whose authority was absolute, but we have only to look at his history in Esther to see that practically all his decisions were made by his ministers, and that he was merely the mouthpiece expressing their judgments. Haman for a time could have his decrees endorsed and signed as though the king had made them himself. The divorce of Vashti, the way a new wife was to be found to take her place, the hanging of Haman, and the permission for the Jews to defend themselves were all matters devised by others and not his personal decisions. Even to this day, many decrees are made by those in authority which are not the fruit of their personal judgment, but the product of the influence of those near to them.

There is one more important purpose of this book which must not be overlooked. It is the insight it gives into the practices and behaviour of worldliness in high places. We all know of kings' palaces, but, as regards the Scriptures, it is only in Esther that the curtain is drawn back and a glimpse afforded us of what life is like in such places. Truly wealth and pomp bring out the worst in fallen man and manifest his lust for fleshly indulgence. Solomon, who knew more of prosperity than most, had to confess that "all is vanity and vexation of spirit". The refusal of Vashti to display her beauty was the fly in the ointment, and left the king in shame and dishonour in spite of the revelry around him. Practically all the pleasure enjoyed in the royal palace was that false pleasure which wine produces.

DIVISIONS OF THE BOOK

Unlike most other books of the Bible, Esther has proved to be most difficult to divide into distinct sections, so most are content to look at it as one continuous story. However, we could view it as having one person prominent in each of its different parts. For example, the king and his wives (chs. 1-2); the exaltation of Haman, and his decree to slay the Jews (chs. 3-5); Mordecai honoured (ch. 6); Esther's successful effort to deliver her people (chs. 6-8); and the Jews' victory with its celebration (chs. 9-10). Admittedly this is not altogether a satisfactory way of dealing with the book, but it is at least an attempt to show the drift of its contents.

THE ADDITIONS IN THE SEPTUAGINT

The Greek translation of the OT commonly known as the Septuagint contains some five additional passages which are wanting in the Hebrew Bible. These were added by a later hand and obviously the motive behind them was to introduce the religious element into what was originally a secular book. In these additions the name of God is freely used: a dream which Mordecai was supposed to have, his prayer, and Esther's prayer, together with more details about Purim were thought to enrich the book and make it more attractive to the Jewish readers. Some minor omissions of the Hebrew text are also noticeable, but these are of little importance. Who added these passages we cannot tell, but they are not authentic, as most scholars agree, so we need not give them undue attention.

KING AHASUERUS AND HIS WIVES
(ch. 1:1 - ch. 2:23)

THE FEAST AT SHUSHAN (1:1-8)

When we open the pages of the Book of Esther we are immediately entering the realm of worldly pomp and grandeur and that of a magnitude which only the heart of a great empire could display. Here in ch. 1 of this rare portion of history we are allowed to penetrate into this domain, and learn while doing so, something of what life in high circles was like in those far off days. In no other part of the OT are we allowed any insight into the behaviour in such exclusive places. Perhaps the nearest to it is the account of the feast of Belshazzar in Dan 5, but it was a passing show which lasted for one night only, whereas the festivities here extended to no less than one hundred and eighty days.

We are satisfied that the Ahasurus named here is the well-known king known in Greek circles as Xerxes, and therefore the son of Darius and grandson of Cyrus. There appears to be little doubt about this, for even the New International Version is so bold as to call him by this Greek name. This being so we can derive from secular sources some understanding of his characteristics and of the conditions obtaining in his realm at this time. Those acquainted with Persian history tell us that he was a cruel despot, who often acted in frenzy as he did at the Hellespont when he ordered three hundred stripes to be inflicted on the waves because they had wrecked his bridges and boats; he also condemned his mechanics to be beheaded because their work had not stood the stress of the storm. In light of these things we need not be surprised if we find in Esther things which he did in haste and without due consideration. One of the difficulties in dealing with the various kings of Persia mentioned in Scripture is that different men are given the same name or appellation. Thus we have two called Cyrus, three called Darius, and three called Ahasuerus. The one we are considering in this book succeeded his father Darius in the year 486 BC and came into the royal line of Cyrus through his mother. He reigned twenty one years, and was murdered by one of his courtiers. He is to be distinguished from the Ahasuerus mentioned in Ezra 4:6 and from the other in Dan 9:1. We can do this on the principle of elimination: he was a real king, and therefore distinct from the Ahasuerus of Dan 9:1; and his having dominion over India distinguishes him from the Ahasuerus of Ezra 4:6, for the realm of the earlier kings of Persia did not extent so far. In the second year of his reign he succeeded in subduing the Egyptians who had revolted against his father. By looking into his history we can learn not only something of the extravagance and lavishness of this great feast, but, what is more important, why it was devised. We are told it was in the king's third year, so it was directly before his impending conflict with the threatening Greek army. Such was the importance of this campaign that he attempted to draw together all the assistance he could muster, even from the most remote parts of his wide empire. In doing so he was seeking to impress the heads of the different provinces of his vast resources and of the wonderful power at his disposal. The NIV translates the end of v. 4: "the military leaders of Persia and Media". If this be correct it confirms the idea that this gathering of these princes was no mere social function. Thus we read, "he showed the riches of his glorious kingdom and the honour of his excellent majesty many days" (v. 4). Any evidence of weakness or of limited supplies would have damped their enthusiasm to join him in the conflict. The long duration of festivity was perhaps needful to allow time for those of them who had to travel from far off places to prepare their retinue and traverse the many miles to Shushan, possibly in chariots or even on the backs of asses. We need not suppose that all these dignities arrived on the first day of the feast, nor that they were a ll present all the time. The explanation in brackets, "this is Ahasuerus which reigned, from India even unto Ethiopia, over a hundred and seven and twenty provinces" (v. 1), is most important for two reasons. First, it identifies which Ahasuerus is being spoken of, for only the son of Darius had such an extensive empire (his father Darius, had only one hundred and twenty provinces), and secondly, it explains why so much time was spent assembling together the princes of all his provinces. If we consider the great image shown to Daniel where the Medo-Persian empire is represented by the breast and arms of silver, it will be obvious that the arms were outstretched, one to reach deep into Africa in the west, and the other to reach as far into Asia as India in the East. Originally, of course, the two arms represented the two partners of the empire, Media and Persia. In the earlier mention of this combined kingdom the name "Mede" is first, whereas in later times "Persia" becomes more prominent. Apparently Shushan was a comparatively new palace and was used mainly as a summer residence for the king. His greatest opponents were the Greeks, who were rising to power at that time, and who, even with a smaller force, were able to defeat his huge army on at least two occasions.

We must bear in mind that the events of this book took place during the "times of the Gentiles", and that these had continued for over a century. It has to be conceded that the lapse of so many years must naturally have resulted in most of the Jews settling down and somewhat adapting their lifestyle so as to feel at home in the lands of their exile. Few, if any of them, would have known by personal experience the importance of the land of their fathers. Doubtless this explains why, throughout this book, there is no mention by them of the house of David, nor is there any reference to their yearning for Jerusalem, the seat of his throne. It also explains why the number who returned home, when free to do so, was so small.

One of the major difficulties of the king was to assure himself of the unity of the empire. With so many nations and so many different peoples, it was not easy for him to keep them all happy together. His predecessors were compelled to quell many uprisings, and to subdue the rebels by stern measures. Ahasuerus, on this occasion, took no chances, and made all the rulers of the provinces feel they had an equal share in the purposed campaign. At this great feast they not only learned the greatness of the empire to which they belonged, but their own importance in maintaining it in its present state. Not that all of them could contribute the same resources for the coming engagement, for some were vast and wealthy while others were comparatively small and poor lands. Sometimes even ungodly men can manifest prudence in the way they handle difficult situations, and can avoid many of the problems which arise amongst the saints as the result of leaders not appreciating the importance of those among them who, though not highly gifted, yet none the less are valuable for the maintenance of the testimony. If men are made to feel that they are a vital part of any campaign, it helps them to throw their full weight into it.

The closing week of the feast was of special significance, for the king arranged that its days would be filled with the enjoyment by all of a magnificent garden party, one which exceeded in lavish entertainment anything previously shared during the many months of festivity. All the guests were made welcome and allowed to indulge without restraint or compulsion in the sumptuous banquet of wine. It is important to note that feasting or banqueting is a key feature of this book, for the original Hebrew word occurs in it no less than nineteen times. It is also well to note the place given to wine in these banquets. Whether the feast was this exceptional one, or the banquet prepared by Esther, we would be led to think that the only item on the menu was wine. Doubtless other commodities were present, but in the story they are passed over as though they were unworthy of mentioning. We might note by way of contrast that when David invited Mephibosheth to dine at his table (2 Sam 9), the stress is on bread, "...thou shalt eat bread at my table continually". This might suggest that the nourishment of the guest was uppermost in the mind of David, but in the mind of the Persian king the most important thing was the merriment of the guests. Most know that wine and wit are seldom in the same person, nevertheless, it is universally acknowledged that those intoxicated are willing to undertake risks that a sober man would hesitate to take. False courage can, however, be dangerous, and many disasters have occurred as the result of the madness intoxication can produce.

The drink, the drapery and the divans at Shushan were all designed to display the wealth of the king, and to give the strangers a taste of the luxuries enjoyed by him. In vvs. 6 - 8 we are told in detail of the delightful surroundings where the guests were feasted. No doubt the curtains were meant to shield from the sun, the couches were for reclining upon when overcome with the wine, and the variety of drinking vessels added diversity to the occasion as they glittered in the sunshine. Apparently a pavement of various coloured stones was laid on part of the garden and this formed a decorative platform on which the couches could rest. Such a mosaic patterned stone floor would help to keep the feet of the guests cool, and thus add to their comfort. The detailed description of the curtains, the couches and the floor is not without interest. Most likely the colours of the curtains were the royal colours (see ch. 8:15), and the material together with the cords by which it was suspended on the marble pillars were made of linen. Whether these curtains were merely hung vertically, or whether they formed a canopy, we are not told, but possibly they formed protection from the elements however used. The amount of gold needed to make the large number of beds or couches sufficient to accommodate the number present, must have been immense, not to speak of the incalculable value of it. In those days this precious metal must have been in good supply. There were four different stones used in the floor, or pavement. They are difficult to identify as their names occur only here; but of this we are sure, they were designed to give the floor the same degree of beauty as was displayed in the curtains, so that no matter which way any guest looked, a pleasant sight greeted his eyes.

Contrary to our expectations, there is no mention here of music, or of singing, or of trumpet-blowing. The Persians seemed to have had little interest in music, nor did the Israelites enjoy it while in captivity; but when they were emancipated and the temple was re-erected in Ezra, and later when the wall was repaired, the singing and music were restored. See especially Neh 12. We might wonder why such specific features are given of all these things, but we may be sure they are meant to let us see what the world esteems as of greatest value. It has not changed from then, for even in this age great store is put upon environment. In hotels and palaces comfortable couches, beautiful floors, (not of mosaic stone, but of deep-piled carpet), heavy curtains to tone, attractive decor, and intoxicating drink, play an important role in the entertainment of present-day society. Indeed, if one of these golden couches were offered for sale today, there would be those who would prize it so much as to give a fabulous price for it. Those of us who, like Solomon, have learned the vanity of the world and its treasures, no longer are allured by such outward displays, for each can sing, "Oh worldly pomp and glory, your charms are spread in vain, I've heard a sweeter story, I've found a truer gain". Those of us who cannot afford worldly grandeur can content ourselves with a simple way of life, whereas those who possess excessive worldly wealth are severely tested. They are in danger of allowing their otherwise favourable circumstances to cause them to abandon their pilgrim character, and to settle down in the world as though it were their home. Quite often the excuse given for lavish living is that all the expense involved can be afforded, and that all accounts have been settled, so nothing unlawful has occurred. However, the standard for the Christian is not to be found in the world, but rather in the Scriptures. Paul reminds us that if we have food and raiment we should be content, and that we ought to be content with such things as we have. He suffered the loss of all things, and One greater than he, the Lord Himself, who was rich, became poor and at times, even during the night, had no roof over His head.

As far as the record goes, this feast differed greatly from the feast of Belshazzar, in which special praise was offered to the gods of gold and silver, and the drinking-vessels used had been stolen from the house of God in Jerusalem. The absence of idolatrous or religious exercises on this occasion is just as strange as the absence of true devotion to God later in the book. In most of the tablets which have been discovered from those ancient days the great victories recorded are attributed to the help of the gods, but this is not the case here. Perhaps the reason is that the deliverance of the Jews, later narrated, would have given the glory to the unseen God of Israel, and it was not expedient for His name to appear in the archives of the Persian empire.

One other feature of this garden fete was the absence of constraint. Nothing is so dear to the heart of man as having his own way, so there was no compulsion either to drink or to abstain. The paramount aim of the king was the pleasure of his guests. They were given their own will for this week, and possibly in the midst of their revelry none of them ever stopped to think that his own people, some years earlier, were among those who had been subjected to the onslaught and tyranny of these same Persians. Their fathers knew more of wickedness and cruel sufferings than they did of wine and surfeiting. The lavish entertainment erased from their minds the memory of this black past. All such sad reflections were out of keeping with this grand banquet. The wine in the stomach had drowned all memories of former sorrows, and elated them with a sense of self-importance. Perhaps not until they arrived at Shushan and listened to the counsel of the princes did they fully realise the plan and purpose of this feast. Little did they conceive that the solemn outcome of the whole affair would be the slaughter by the Greeks of many of their subjects. The mustering of all the forces of the empire was essential for the great engagement soon to be undertaken by the proud king, and, sad to say, the ultimate outcome was that many thus recruited filled early graves.

VASHTI REFUSES THE KING'S DEMAND (1:9 - 12)

While the banquet of the king was proceeding, another one was organised by the queen for the entertainment of the women. The visitors most likely brought their wives with them, and possibly some of the children, so these would not be permitted to share in the secrets dealt with in the counsel of war organised by the king. Doubtless the ladies were quite happy to have their own good time away from the terror and uncertainty of the inner court. However, on the last day of the feast, when the senses of the king had been blunted by drinking too much wine, he thought how wonderful it would be if these princes and his lords could see the beauty of his partner. He imagined this would be the highlight of the occasion, and would demonstrate to his nobles the good taste that he had, even in his choice of a queen. She was to appear in all her royal apparel, and her head adorned with the royal crown. Had his plan succeeded, the applause of his princes would have thrilled his heart, for she would have shown them the most perfect example of beauty they had ever beheld. Alas! to his bitter disappointment and to the amazement of all present, she bluntly refused to obey his orders. He had spared no effort in making sure his message was delivered to her by the choicest of his chamberlains, so that no excuse could be found for not considering the request as important. Well would she know, when she saw the band of no less than seven chief men approaching, that something of great importance must be in their mission. Nevertheless, she dared to refuse the call, and continued to enjoy herself in her own private banquet.

We are not surprised that the great embarrassment and the shame of being refused, aroused the rage of the king: "therefore was the king very wroth, and his anger burned in him" (v. 12), for he had been not only let down but humiliated in the presence of those whose esteem he most valued, and that at the time when he most expected to be extolled to the highest heights. Most can bear being let down privately, or even if the secret is shared by only a few, but when the heads of a vast empire all witness the disgrace then the feelings in the heart are beyond expression. She, who was the apple of his eye, because of this action had become the fly in his ointment. Her disobedience brought to light the weakness of the most powerful man upon earth. The one who posed to be competent to rule the greatest empire in the world at that time, was proved incapable of ruling his own home, and that before a host of witnesses. Had she been asked to do the impossible her refusal could have been understood, but she could have fulfilled the king's demand without in any way bringing dishonour upon herself. Such downright rebellion was foreign to the Persian court, and must have amazed her own guests, even as it did all who surrounded the king. It could well be that she too was in some measure intoxicated, and that this gave her false courage to do what no queen would ever have dreamed of doing. In the providence of God the grand show ended in disaster, and all the pleasures so successfully enjoyed until now were displaced by anger and bitterness. Unknown to the king and his princes this humiliation was a preview of the more serious dishonour which was in store for him and them when they would be heavily defeated by the threatening Greek army. This is the first of several occasions in this book when wrath or anger was manifested in the palace. (See 3:5; 5:9; 7:7.)

As already pointed out in the introduction, a noted feature in this book is the way its characters suffer sudden reverses from heights to valleys throughout its pages. Here is the first of these, and more will follow. In this part of the story we can learn that sometimes the enjoyments of the world are marred by disappointments. Even those in the best possible circumstances, and possessing without limit all that men count valuable, are taught how unexpectedly they can be brought to the dust. It is well that the believer can be confident that his hope will not make him ashamed. In letting go the world he is not losing much, for all that it has to offer cannot satisfy its own, who live for it; how much less can it give him a true portion, or anything to compare with his treasures which are in heaven. Worldlings like to think that they can gratify every longing of their hearts, and do so without any impediment; but they are not as wise as they ought to be in this assumption, for quite often their schemes are thwarted, and that at the moment when they expect them to be fulfilled.

THE DIVORCE OF VASHTI (1:13 - 22)

Not until the king was in difficulty do we learn how much he was dependent upon his advisers. He did sit on the throne, and he did wear the crown, but practically all the decisions of the kingdom were made by his seven councillors. These formed an inner cabinet and had personal contact with him. The insult by Vashti had not only hurt the king personally, it had struck a serious blow at his authority in the empire. He could scarcely expect to be obeyed in the wider sphere if he were not master in the smaller sphere of the home. Paul asks the question, "If a man know not how to rule his own house, how shall he take care of the church of God?"

These counsellors were in no doubt that this distressing matter would become known throughout the provinces, for it occurred at the time when all of them were represented by their chiefs, who were assembled at Shushan. The queen had set a precedent which would be copied in every corner of the kingdom, and thus the law established from creation's day, that men should bear rule in their own houses, would be annulled. The sentence decided upon Vashti by the ministers and confirmed by the king was very heavy, for she was not only to be deprived of all contact with the king, but someone else was to take her place. There was no one to speak on her behalf, nor was any provision made for her forgiveness. The die was cast, and her fate was sealed. Who can measure the depths of her despair when at length it dawned upon her what her fate was to be? All know that it is no small trial to be demoted from being queen to the depths of disgrace and poverty. In order to frustrate the development of the evil example she had set, a strong effort was put in motion to re-establish the dignity of the king in his palace, and of all men in his kingdom in their homes. The decree, officially signed, was dispatched to every corner of the empire. It declared "that every man shall bear rule in his own house". Lest any should fail to understand its wording because of language difficulties, it was circulated in the different languages of every people. The closing statement of the chapter, "that it should be published according to the language of every people", is not without its difficulties. Most seem to understand it as an additional command for each man to speak his own language in his own home. Thus, if his wife was a foreigner she must learn his language and all his household must have one speech. In this he would be establishing his authority in his own house. If the wife were to speak a different language and the children learned only from her, as happened in Judea where the children did not know the Hebrew tongue which their fathers spoke (Neh 13:24), this would establish her authority and diminish the authority of the head of the house.

There is an important lesson in this part of the story of Esther in that it illustrates the setting aside of the Gentiles in order to bring the Jews into prominence. The latter had lost their supremacy among the nations because of their disobedience to God, and because Vashti had disobeyed her earthly master she likewise was humiliated. Disobedience in the Garden has brought in a flood of sorrows, and insubjection to divine rule is a root cause of great disasters. It is amazing that God should allow this great upset at the feast in the capital of the supreme empire of that time, to be the occasion for setting in motion the machinery whereby He would exalt His own people in the person of Esther, their representative. Of this we are sure, that when Ahasuerus summoned the nobles to his palace, he had not the slightest idea of the issues which would follow. Uppermost in his mind was his pending battle with the Greeks, but God was working in His own secret way to fulfil His purpose. We might imagine that the worldly affairs pass unnoticed by God, and that He allows everything to proceed as it will; but in this we are mistaken, for there is not a move made by the nations but He has not only knowledge of it but also control of it. The day will come when the "times of the Gentiles" will come to an end, and once again the Jew will rise to the head of the nations; but there will be many upheavals in the world before that comes to pass.

ESTHER IS MADE QUEEN (2:1 - 18)

The counsel of the advisers of Ahasuerus had not only told him to dispose of Vashti, but to "give her royal estate to another that is better than she" (1:19). This chapter proceeds to show how this was accomplished. However, before we look at this vital part of the story we must look at the time when this great event took place, for we are told that it occurred in the tenth month of the seventh year of the king's reign (2:16). So, what reads like a continuous story, has an interruption of some four years. It will be recalled that the great feast of ch. 1 was held in the third year of the king (1:3). The history of the times solves the problem of the delay, for these years allow time for the great conflict between the Persians and the Greeks, referred to earlier, to take place. In spite of the intense preparations and the excessive numbers of his army, Ahasuerus was shamefully defeated. Some of his mad acts during this campaign, such as ordering the lashing of the waves of the sea, have been the subject of ridicule for generations. It seems to be a feature of the great emperors of the past to make much of their successes in the records they stored, and to pass over, almost in silence, their defeats. If, as we have suggested in our introduction, the Book of Esther was copied from the annals, this would account for the absence of any explanation of the gap in the time scale. While the battle raged and the king was away from his own land he had little time to think of replacing Vashti, but as soon as he returned to his luxurious palace the vacancy, caused by the absence of the queen, would be keenly felt. It could well be that he had some regrets about what he had done, and that he would like to have brought her back, but as usual in Persia he had not the power to reverse the decree of his counsellors. Of this we may be sure, no time was lost in procuring a queen, and thus restoring the kingdom to normality.

The king's servants were quick to advise him as to how he should gratify the longings of his heart. Their plan was to call another great assemblage from all the provinces to the palace at Shushan, but this time fair young girls were to be gathered together, not the nobles as in ch. 1. The aim was to find the most beautiful maiden in the land, and the one who would be most appealing to the king. We might call this a beauty contest, but it was far from a trifling matter as the rest of the story will show. It is a feature of the world that natural beauty is of supreme importance in the choice of a wife. It fails to realise that "Fairest flowers soon decay, youth and beauty pass away", and, what is more important, that character and virtue remain long after outward appearance has changed.

At this juncture a new person enters the story, and one who will play an important role in the rest of this book; his name is Mordecai. He was a son of Jair, and his great-grandfather had been carried down to Babylon at the time when Jeconiah was taken there. (Some have attempted to make the "who" of v. 6 refer to Mordecai, but this would make him over one hundred and twenty years old and his cousin over seventy, so obviously it refers as we have said to his great-grandfather.) He was carried down about eight years after the captivity of Daniel, and about eleven years before Jerusalem was finally destroyed. His genealogy is traced back to the tribe of Benjamin. Some of the names of his forebears here given might suggest that he was related to king Saul, but this idea must be discarded. The chief purpose in mentioning his fathers is to make clear that he was a true Israelite, or Jew as they are called in this book. The name his father gave him seems to have some link with Merodach the Babylonian god, but may have been chosen, as names often are, without any thought of its original meaning. His people had been about one hundred years in captivity by this time, so it is the more surprising that he was not prepared to fit into all the demands of those in power in Persia. It would seem that he was considerably older than his cousin Esther, for she had been reared under his guardianship and was treated by him as his own daughter.

When we reach v. 7 of our chapter we have the first

mention of Esther, the one from whom the book received its name, and the one who will play a major part in the events which will follow. Like not a few who have succeeded in their life's activities, she had the misfortune of being bereft of her parents while she was quite young, so as an orphan she was indebted to her faithful cousin to care for her throughout her tender years. Originally she had a Hebrew name *Hadassah* which means "myrtle", but this was changed to the Persian name *Esther* which means a "star". However, God granted to her the favour of natural beauty, which was to be His way of bringing her into a position of vital importance. In some respects she reminds us of Moses, for he too was born under trying conditions, he too was a beautiful child, he too entered the king's palace, and he too was instrumental in delivering his people.

What in most lands would be the betrothal period was at Shushan a year-long period of preparation, not of one chosen maiden, but of a number from among which one was to be chosen. Amongst the number assembled was Esther the beautiful Jewess, but the identity of her people was not disclosed at this time. A specially selected chamberlain was put in charge of these girls, and was responsible to oversee their purification. This word "purification" occurs only in this passage and in Prov 20:30. The idea behind it was the developing in them, as far as was humanly possible, of all the natural qualities which would make them most attractive to the king. No expense was to be counted too great, nor attention considered too much, so long as the desired end was achieved. The moral standard of all this is never questioned in this book, nor is there any protest mooted against it. Everything is recorded as normal procedure, and as though it were altogether beyond reproach. None of these maidens was asked did she desire to be queen, nor was any father asked would he give his daughter to the king. The feelings of a devout Jewess in having to leave the religion of her fathers and associate with idolatrous practices is never given a thought. The maidens were treated as chattels, and were viewed as being in existence for the pleasure of the king.

The story, as in chapter one, gives us an insight into conditions in the world at that time, and we have already compared them with the present world. In this part of the story we can see another reflection of this present evil age. Where the Word of God is absent and His claims ignored the moral standard is dragged to the lowest depths. Especially in high circles the idea established at Creation of one man having one wife is practically abolished. There are problems in our minds in understanding how a relationship between Esther and the king brought about in this way could be used by God in the fulfilment of His purpose. We might equally have difficulty in understanding that in the genealogy of Christ, as given by Matthew, we have no less than three women mentioned who we would think were unworthy of inclusion. "Thamar" and "the wife of Urias" were both stained with immorality, and "Ruth" was a Moabitess, yet all three had a part in the line which led to Christ. The lesson we must learn is that God fulfils His purpose in spite of human depravity; at the same time and equally we must realise that the fact that He does so in no way justifies the perpetration of evil, nor does it indicate any change in His hatred of it.

Hegai, the chamberlain in charge of the girls, had little difficulty in detecting something of outstanding beauty in Esther, for he showed her special favour and provided her with a retinue of no less than seven maidens. She was also granted the privilege of living in the choicest place of the residence, so that nothing would annoy her or make her feel uncomfortable. From almost the outset of this beauty-contest she was judged by him, and indeed by all who saw her, to be the most likely winner. In the end his discernment proved to be closely in keeping with that of the king himself. That year must have proved very boring for her, and its days must have been filled with apprehension as to what the ultimate outcome would be.

At the end of twelve months' preparation the day came when Esther was brought to the king. This was, without doubt, the most momentous day in her life. Unlike her fellow-maidens, who most likely would seek to impress the king with what they brought with them, she was content to leave that matter to the judgment of Hegai, so, without any special decorations or ornamentation, she was presented to the king. He was immediately enamoured with her, he loved her (the only occasion when love is mentioned in the book), she obtained favour in his sight, and he put the royal crown upon her head. To mark the occasion he made a great banquet for his nobles, so that they might share with him the joy of the occasion. Those who were not brought to the feast were given a holiday, so the whole empire was allowed to celebrate the crowning of the new queen.

The wonder of the world had taken place, for this was probably the first and only time that a Jewess was queen of Persia. It was one thing for Solomon to bring Gentile women into his harem, it was quite another for a Persian monarch to make the daughter of an enslaved nation, and she a Jewess, the queen of his empire. In fairness we must add that he was totally unaware of Esther's nationality, for she had not disclosed the identity of her people. In her case there was also great unawareness as to why she had been raised to such honour, but she would learn later that the role she was being called upon to play would bring with it not only great exaltation but also heavy responsibilities.

The story of how a humble maiden was exalted to such a high position in the world's greatest empire may seem like a fairy tale or petty novel, but there is a side to it that those acquainted with the OT cannot help but view with wonder. It is the fact that here we have a Jewess being forcibly married to a heathen king, to a man who was not only an idolater but also a licentious drunkard. As mentioned earlier, not a word appears in the whole episode regarding the morality or otherwise of what has occurred. It was never God's intention that His people should be united with the heathen, especially when those to whom they unite remain in their evil state. However, it is in keeping with this strange book that such matters as religion and morals do not appear on its pages. It is interesting to see that though Esther was exalted to the position of queen, yet she respected Mordecai, the man who had reared her, and showed this by obeying him, whatever he told her to do. Apparently the Jews were regarded as the most unworthy of all the captives in Persia, so his advice to her was that she should not reveal her people, nor her links with him, the door-man of the palace.

When God works some great deliverance we cannot help being surprised at His achievements, but we should wonder no less how He can set the stage for what none but Himself knows is approaching. Not one in Persia, whether heathen or Jew, had the slightest idea as to why Esther was where she was. Provision for emergencies can be made by God before they arise. In His own wisdom, and often in a way we least expect, He can mysteriously have His plans made, and the wherewithal to fulfil them, and can do so without man detecting what He is doing. The ram in the thicket (Gen 22), the new jaw bone of an ass (Jud 15) and the fish to swallow Jonah (Jonah 1), were no coincidences of nature, but were the provisions of God ready to hand when needed. If we knew Him better, perhaps much of the excitement, and at times panic, which marks us in an emergency would be entirely absent. On not a few occasions the disciples were in great straits to know what to do, but the Lord was calm, for the solution was already known to Him, and He was ever conscious of His Father's providing hand. The lad, when making up the barley bread and the fish for his lunch, could not have foreseen the use to which it eventually would be put, but at length all became clear when the thousands were filled with it (John 6).

A CONSPIRACY UNCOVERED (2:19 - 23)

In the closing three verses of this chapter Mordecai becomes prominent, and not only counsels Esther, but uncovers a conspiracy to murder the king. Most likely because of his relationship with the queen, his cousin, he was privileged to sit in the king's gate. From that vantage point he could watch what was transpiring in the court, and learn secrets that those less privileged would never discover. During this time a plot was laid by Bigthana and Teresh to assassinate the king. Little would he suspect that the two men he had appointed to guard the doorway of his palace would conspire to murder him. However, there was one man in his kingdom who could be trusted, and he not only learned of their evil design but, through Esther, conveyed the news of it to the king. The result of this was that the two evil men were hanged on a gallows.

It is a feature of life that often days of rejoicing are followed by days of adversity. Had these two men succeeded in their design they would have quickly ended the king's honeymoon, and at the same moment dashed to the ground all the bright hopes which Esther had in her new-found partner. There is in this short episode another lesson. God was teaching the Gentile world its need of the despised Jew. At the same time Mordecai was fulfilling the injunction of Jeremiah that the people who were carried into captivity were to seek the welfare of the land of their adoption. His words were, "Seek the peace of the city whither I have caused you to be carried away captives" (Jer 29:7). Whether Mordecai was acting out of the spirit of duty or obeying the prophet we may not know, but of this we are sure, his righteous intervention on the king's behalf paid good dividends as we shall later see.

In this early day of Esther's entering her high position she became the channel of communication between Mordecai and the king. Her experience at this time was a kind of preview of what she would later have to do. Little did she imagine that the day would come when the threat of death would be not on the king but on herself and her people, and that again she would be the intermediary between Mordecai and the king. We must note that there was no immediate reward granted to Mordecai for his saving the life of Ahasuerus. God in His overruling hand kept this back until the time when it fulfilled His purpose in humiliating Haman and exalting the despised Jew. Another important link between this and the later story is that the two men who sought the king's life were hanged, so too were Haman and his sons when the plot they devised was discovered and judged.

This glimpse into the treachery that existed in Shushan teaches us the solemn lesson that men in high places in the world are very insecure. They never know what evil is planned against them, nor how soon all that seems precious can be taken from them. How different are the saints, for all they are promised is secure: their inheritance is incorruptible and eternal in the heavens. As has been often pointed out,

Daniel slept more soundly in the den of lions than the king did in his bed. We can also learn that the world owes a debt to the despised Jew. Even as far back as the days of Joseph, the Egyptian empire was saved from starvation by his wisdom. In the purposes of God the seed of Abraham has been a blessing to mankind, in spite of the fact that they have often been in painful conditions because of their sin against Him. The crowning blessings of all have come to the world through Christ, who also was of the seed of Abraham, and who also was despised and rejected.

HAMAN THE JEWS' ENEMY
(ch. 3:1 - ch. 4:3)

MORDECAI REFUSES TO ACKNOWLEDGE HAMAN
(3:1 - 4)

Had the story ended with chapter 2 all would have appeared to be well with the captives in Persia, for one of their number was queen of the land. But as ever in this book, the sun is no sooner risen than the black clouds appear. Some time seems to have elapsed between the events of the previous chapter and the commencement of this one. This is implied in the words, "After these things". A new personage comes before us here, one who will play a leading role in the next few chapters of this strange story. He was called Haman, which some think means "magnificent", and was an Agagite. Although he was not the king, yet as far as influence and power were concerned he exerted these to an extent far beyond what we would have expected. All he needed to do was to make the proposals, and like an obedient child the king would endorse them without question.

Just as a brief statement of Mordecai's ancestry is given in 2:5 where he is said to be the son of Shimei, the son of Kish, so here we are told that Haman was the son of Hammedatha the Agagite. The similarity of these names to those mentioned in the history of Saul and David has led some to think that Mordecai was a descendant of Shimei, the man who cursed David, and that Haman was a descendant of Agag whom Saul spared. However, while appealing to our minds as teaching some helpful lessons, this is not true to fact. There is little doubt that Haman is a Persian name, as also is that of his father, Hammedatha.

If it is in any way legitimate to view Mordecai as God's

representative in a heathen land, we can also with little difficulty see in Haman the hallmarks of Satan. In every movement in the story the traces of the archenemy can be discovered. We have already surveyed with wonder how God had overruled in bringing one of His earthly, and at this time degraded, people into a place of high honour, but He is not the only person interested in the nation, for Satan too has his eye upon it, and will do all in his power to thwart the purposes of God concerning it. The Jews in Persia were of little importance, so much so that the king scarcely knew of their existence; yet they were not left without divine help. On the other hand, we might wonder why the enemy should be so opposed to them, seeing they were so down-trodden and therefore so helpless to upset his sway over the millions of people who filled the Persian empire. The lesson being taught is one of long standing, for ever since the Lord put Adam and Eve into the Garden the same enemy has ceaselessly wrought to destroy the handiwork of God. If God has His instruments whom He uses to fulfil His purpose, so Satan also is quick to find someone who will willingly do his evil work.

There is another aspect to these strange matters which we do well to bear in mind, for just as God raised up Pharaoh that His power might be displayed in Egypt, so God allowed Haman to appear on the scene at this time that the sovereignty of His hand might be made known in Persia. We must also point out that these places where such manifestations of power were granted, were theatres otherwise in the dark as to the great Creator. The bondage of Israel in Egypt and the captivity of the Jews in Persia were not altogether without good results, for they served divine purposes in that they were turned to opportunities for the display of God's might and glory.

The exaltation of Haman to a position next to the king,

and to a seat on a throne (the word "seat" (v. 1) is normally translated "throne"), no doubt inflamed his natural pride and put into his heart the desire for divine honours. So lofty was he that all the officials who administered the king's business were willing to bow before him and give him their devoted homage. The aim of Satan has ever been to obtain divine honour and to be "like the most High", so we need not be surprised if his puppets follow his example. Even in the Tribulation times the same principle will apply, for the Antichrist will sit "in the temple of God, showing himself that he is God" (2 Thess 2:4). The first beast of Rev 13, the head of the revived Roman Empire, will likewise claim divine honours; and his subordinate, the second beast, will assist him in obtaining these. It would appear that when Haman was demanding the worship of all the servants at Shushan he was not going beyond what was sanctioned by the king, so if any refused him his homage he was not only insulting him but also refusing to obey the king. In light of this we can see the gravity of Mordecai's attitude and the enormity of the risk he was taking. Little wonder that the other servants exclaimed to him, "Why transgressest thou the king's commandment?" (v. 3). Unless there was some deep and serious reason for his stubbornness, what he was failing to do was nothing short of rebellion, and that of a public nature. He who had acted with such tact and wisdom in advising Esther in her advancement to queenship must never be viewed as a foolhardy play-actor, but as a humble and sincere man who sought to do what was right in the sight of God and men. His refusal to bow is explained to the king's servant by a simple confession that he was a Jew. This open witness to the identity of his people is in sharp contrast to his advice to Esther, for he had charged her not to show her kindred nor her people (2:10,20). Perhaps this very crisis was God's sovereign way of bringing to light the identity of His testimony-bearer in that dark land. We might well ask, "Why should being a Jew make any difference in the matter of bowing at the king's command?" The answer is clear: although he had been born and reared in a foreign land Mordecai was no Persian, neither nationally nor religiously. Lingering in his soul was the grand truth, "Thou shalt have no other gods before me". In light of this he could not bow the knee to a self-appointed god, even though in refusing to do so he risked not only Haman's wrath but also the wrath of Ahasuerus. Like Daniel before him, his conscientious objections could not be forfeited whatever be the cost. Daniel refused not to bow the knee and pray to God; here Mordecai refused to bow the knee to a mere mortal man. Both men were brought to the point of death for their faithfulness, but God delivered both out of their plight. Often there is much blame laid at the door of those in captivity who refused the offer of Cyrus to return to their own land, but while this is deserved, we cannot fail to admire the faithfulness here displayed at Shushan by a lonely individual, one who might have escaped much sorrow if he had only conformed to the pattern around him. Such fidelity must have given pleasure to God, but no reference to this could appear in this book.

The practical application of this short passage is of great importance in our day. Not a few of the saints find themselves in situations where they must either take a stand for the Lord, or else go against their conscience and grieve Him. The Christian child at school, especially if far from home, may be tempted when asked to engage in matters totally contrary to his or her conscience. To refuse can be costly, but, if done in a humble spirit, can be a wonderful testimony. The Christian businessman can be tempted into the snare of an unequal yoke by being forced into some combine, unless like Mordecai he takes his stand and refuses to disobey the Word of God. Some have even bowed to the unequal yoke in matrimony with the excuse that no Christian partner was available. What we need to see is that such tests are golden opportunities for the believer to declare his relationship to the Lord, and to show how much he values this relationship. God did not fail Mordecai, neither will He fail His faithful ones in this day.

HAMAN'S PLOT TO DESTROY THE JEWS (3:5 - 6)

Perhaps nothing can be more painful to a man in a high position than the wounding of his pride. We might think that the death of Mordecai should have been enough to assuage the wrath of the offended courtier, but alas, no such limit entered the head of this madman. Only the wiping out of the entire Jewish population throughout the extent of the empire could suffice to satisfy his rage. The faithful stand of one man put the lives of all his people in jeopardy. By confessing that he was a Jew, and that this was the grounds for his refusal to bow, he had given some basis to Haman for destroying all who shared his belief. Naturally Haman concluded that every Jew would resist his demands, and that the slaying of one of them would not obliterate this problem.

THE FINDING OF THE DATE (3:7)

We have already noticed the absence of all religious activity throughout the book of Esther, but if it is absent, we learn that superstition was not. To our amazement the raging prince sought by lot to find the exact date on which to begin his onslaught on the Jews. Apparently he believed in some super power which could direct him to what he would have thought was his lucky day. In the account of this performance we learn that it occurred in the twelfth year of king Ahasuerus, so Esther at this time would have been married four years. This period would have been sufficient to allow her to settle into her position as queen, and to feel at home in the enjoyments of the palace with all its retinue of servants. Little did she realise how quickly all would change, and that the shock of her life was lingering at the door.

In Proverbs we read, "The lot is cast into the lap; but the whole disposing thereof is of the Lord" (16:33). If ever there was a clear example of this, it was on this occasion. Once more we are seeing in this book the sovereignty of God. How strange, yet not strange, that the lot did not decide the date until the twelfth month, so that almost a whole year was to run by from the time the sentence was passed until the time of its execution. By thus delaying the destruction of the Jews, God was allowing time for the wicked plan to be overruled and His people to be delivered. All the Jews, from the queen down to the lowest in the land, were made to endure the most distressing twelve months they ever experienced. Many of them might well have wished Mordecai had not brought them into such a strait, but nothing they could do or say would lift the black cloud from off them.

The episode in Persia is a faint picture of the great Tribulation which awaits the Jews after the Church is raptured. It will last for three and one half years, so will be a much longer period than the one with which we are dealing. Those who will refuse the mark of the beast, and like Mordecai refuse to bow, in many cases will have to pay the supreme penalty, but at the end the Lord will deliver at His coming all who will have survived the storm. The time of Jacob's trouble will seem long and dreary, but the faithful will soon forget their sorrows when their tears are dried, and their song of deliverance begins. Most of God's people find life a mixture of joy and sorrow. Days of blessing and prosperity are often followed by times of distress and anguish. The more faithful testimony-bearers would appear to be the more tested, and at times they wonder why all the trials come their way, but just as deliverance came to the distressed Jews, so too will it be enjoyed by the saints in this age. One thing is sure, Mordecai could never have foreseen how deliverance would come; nor yet shall we until it has been granted.

HAMAN OBTAINS THE CONSENT OF THE KING
(3:8 - 11)

In order to carry out his wicked plan Haman must obtain the sanction of the king. He acquired this in a crafty and deceitful way, by putting before him two main propositions. First, he told him there was a people in his realm who were not only diverse from all others but were rebellious against his laws. Secondly, he promised that he would deposit all the spoils of these people in the king's treasury. The two most powerful levers were therefore brought into play upon the king's mind. Every ruler hates to have a rebel people in his kingdom, and likewise every ruler values highly all that will enrich his coffers. Without further ado or question the matter was settled. The decree was not only signed, but the ring which sealed all official documents was handed to Haman, so that thereafter he could endorse with it any decree he wished to make. Such decrees were unalterable according to the laws of the Medes and Persians.

With a seat on a throne, the king's ring on his hand, and every device of his mind going according to plan, Haman must have been a happy man. He had reached the pinnacle of his glory, and had all the cravings of his proud heart gratified. Alas! in his short-sightedness he could not foresee that in this very successful negotiation he was signing his own death-warrant. The king, likewise, failed to realise that the decree he had sanctioned involved his closest and dearest, his bosom companion, the queen herself. Crafty and clever men often show the shallowness of their thinking when dealing with matters involving the people of God. "The secret of the Lord is with them that fear him", means that often those whom the world thinks are simple prove to be more wise than the wiseacres who despise them. Joseph, for example, was able to teach the senators of Egypt wisdom, and Daniel had more wisdom than all the Chaldeans of Babylon.

The success, especially at the outset, of the most evil of devices has always been a puzzle to the thoughtful believer. He imagines that the best thing that could happen is that God would nip in the bud every unrighteous plan, and save His people from all the distress they suffer before He grants them deliverance. Quite often the expected deliverance is not granted until despair fills the hearts of those who are waiting. One great reason for this is that God is so powerful that He can afford to allow His enemies to prevail even until almost the last moment. Those who are contending with an enemy as strong as themselves must try to land a decisive blow as soon as possible, for if the fight is prolonged it may mean their defeat. Not so with the Almighty, for He can sit in the heavens and laugh at the vain attempts of His foes who are so foolish as to imagine they are about to triumph. A second reason for His working in this way is that He develops in His own a knowledge of Himself. Every experience and every crisis through which they pass leads them further along the path of faith, and therefore increases their confidence in Him.

THE NEWS OF THE DECREE DISPATCHED
(3:12 - 15)

No time was lost by Haman in having the notice of the decree spread to ever corner of the vast empire. There appears to have been no shortage of scribes at Shushan, for on the thirteenth day of the first month all was written and sealed. The posting of so many copies was a major task, for each copy had to be delivered by hand. The distance to some of the remote parts of the kingdom was very long, and due to the absence of mechanised transport must have taken quite a time to cover. However, there was no need for such a rush, for eleven months would pass before the execution of its demands had to be met.

The wording of the important document is given in v. 13. The three terms used, "to destroy", "to kill", and "to cause to perish" indicate the complete ruin of the Jews. They were not only to be killed, but their entire estate was to be annihilated. The second point in it demanding the destruction of them was likewise to be universal. Neither root nor branch was to remain, so even the little children were to be slain. The third feature of it was that all their possessions were to be forfeited and collected as a prey. This would not only cover the cost of the operation, but add a surplus to the king's treasury.

Some can easily understand why Satanic devices were directed against the children of Abraham and their annihilation attempted, for they see in this the evil one's design to prevent the coming of the promised Messiah, Abraham's seed. The destruction of the male children in Egypt, and the almost complete destruction of the royal line of David at a later time (2 Kings 11:1) can be quoted as further examples. But what is surprising in this story is that although there was no hope of Christ arising from any of the Jews in captivity, yet the same evil principle was in operation. The answer to this anomaly lies in the fact that Israel was God's chosen people, and as such had to share the consequences of the perpetual hatred of His arch-enemy. Just as the Christian in this age shares the reproach of Christ, so the Jews in Persia had to suffer because they belonged to God.

We can scarcely imagine the shock that must have 'rocked the Jewish communities when the news reached them of their impending fate. The city of Shushan, being the seat of power and the original source of the plot, was naturally the first place to be stirred with the news. While all was well with the king and Haman as they sat together drinking, the people outside were "perplexed". Neither Persian nor Jew could disentangle the serious matter, for the like had never before been heard of in their land. An insight into the callousness of Haman's heart is revealed in his indifference to the sorrow and suffering he designed to bring to the many Jews, almost all of whom he had never seen nor known. "The tender mercies of the wicked are cruel" (Prov 12:10), and this cruelty is an exhibition of the character of the devil who energises them, for "he was a murderer from the beginning" (John 8:44).

MORDECAI AND THE JEWS MOURN (4:1 - 3)

One of the first to learn of the impending disaster was Mordecai, for being at the palace and being privy to all that transpired there, meant that the decree was no sooner signed than he was told about it. In a certain sense he was responsible for all the distress that was befalling his people, for had he bowed to Haman all would have been as usual with them. Adopting the garb of mourning, and going out into the most public place to lament and cry, he left nobody in Shushan in any doubt about the seriousness of the situation. Had he been allowed he would almost certainly have ventured into the palace itself, but because his sackcloth disqualified him from entering, he stopped at the gate. His position was close enough to the palace to cause the news to penetrate where his feet could not go. The constant passing in and out of the queen's retinue meant that they witnessed his distress, and no doubt reported it to her majesty. As the news of the decree spread throughout the city and further afield, much grief came with it, so sackcloth and wailing were the order of the day for all the Jews.

As we have already pointed out, this bitter experience is but a faint picture of that distress that will be experienced by the Jews of the future during the "time of Jacob's trouble" (Jer 30:7). In all other times of distress the nation had some source of comfort, for they had the priesthood and the prophets. Whether we think of the time in Babylon, or the time when the remnant returned, or even look to the future, God ever provides spiritual help to His people, but at Shushan there was apparently not a word from God, nor a sign of His hand to be seen. To all who viewed them outwardly, the Jews appeared to be deserted by their God, even by Him whom Mordecai had sought to honour.

Whether the Jewish captives kept in segregated areas or freely mixed amongst the population we are not told, but this much is clear, in spite of the years they were away from their own land they had not lost their identity. Most other nations become absorbed into the population in which they are made to dwell, and in a matter of less than a century they can be no longer distinguished as a people. This is specially true when there is no colour barrier. In all organised persecutions of the Jews, even to this day, there never appears to have been any difficulty in identifying them.

ESTHER AND THE DECREE
(ch. 4:4 - ch. 7:10)

ESTHER LEARNS OF THE DECREE (4:4 - 9)

In spite of luxurious surroundings and unlimited service, Esther was sufficiently human to feel sorely grieved for the distress of her devoted cousin. When the news reached her of his standing in the street dressed in mourner's apparel, she, in her simplicity, thought to relieve the situation by providing him with a change of garments. Her offer was refused, because wearing different clothes would not have touched the true cause of his grief, but would only have covered the expression of it.

When the queen's maids returned to her with the refused clothes she then realised that something very serious was troubling Mordecai, so without delay she sent Hatach, her trusted servant, to ascertain the facts. These he obtained without difficulty, for he was not only told of the cause of the lamentation, but was given a copy of Haman's decree which was in the hand of Mordecai. Obviously the man who commenced the trouble would be one of the first to receive a copy of the decree dealing with it. This document removed all doubt from Esther's mind as to the seriousness of the threat. Never before had she read such a distressing composition, for she could see clearly the extent of the slaughter, not only of Mordecai, but of all Jews. She may not have disclosed her nationality to the king, but nevertheless she could not forget that the people under this threat were her own people and kindred. If it were executed and she spared, she would be the only Jew alive in all the empire. The horror of the hour must have been beyond description, and a sense of helplessness must have possessed her soul.

The close of the message sent to Esther brought to her

the responsibility she had in trying to have this terrible disaster averted. She was the only Jew on earth who had access to the king, so to her alone could Mordecai turn for help. He charged her to go in to the king and intercede for him and his people. In his message he gave no thought to the enormity of his demand, but looked upon the fulfilment of it as well within the scope of her normal life. Upon us, who read the story, the fact is beginning to dawn that it was the providence of God which had her where she was. Possibly the thought did not occur to her that her call to be queen had this very crisis in view. Some four years earlier God, by His overruling hand, had made provision for the emergency which now arose. He had His instruments in place before they were needed, so what appeared to man to be an impossible situation, to Him was just something which He had already anticipated. Perhaps one of the great failings of many is that they fail to grasp what they are capable of doing. It never entered Esther's mind that she was the one person on earth who could save her people at this time. Even Moses was slow to believe that he was the instrument God had prepared to go to Pharaoh and deliver Israel from slavery. There is a danger of overestimating our ability, but there is a far greater possibility that we underestimate it. It is strange that her cousin had to tell Esther what she could do at this time; she herself was totally unaware of it, and even when told seemed reluctant enough to believe that it was within her reach.

ESTHER'S REPLY (4:10 - 12)

The message, which was perfectly reasonable from the sender's point of view, was far from welcomed by the queen. Whether or not Mordecai knew the etiquette of the palace we are not told, but her reply made abundantly clear the stark reality of the danger that would be involved in fulfilling his request. For her or anyone else to venture into the king's presence uninvited was nothing short of a serious risk of life. Moreover, for reasons she did not know, a month had passed without a single invitation coming to her from the king. This absence of friendship intensified her fears that the worst would befall her if she dared to appear before him. Perhaps Haman had so occupied the king with entertainment and banquets of wine, that he had little thought of the queen, or interest in her company. We need not doubt that the crafty enemy of the Jews would try to prevent the king from giving the decree serious thought and possibly changing his mind about what he had sanctioned. This practice of allowing only those invited to have an audience with the king may seem strange to us, but when we recall that the life of the king was ever in danger, not from the distant foes but from those in close proximity to him, we can appreciate the care he needed to exercise in this matter. Even with all his precautions he was eventually murdered by one of his own courtiers.

MORDECAI'S SECOND MESSAGE (4:13 - 14)

If Esther thought that because of the peril she would face by going to the king she would be excused from further action she was gravely mistaken, for the second message sent to her left her with little option but to face the danger and plead for her people. This message had three important elements in it. First, she was shown that she would be put to death like all the other Jews, for there was no exemption for any in the decree; so she was going to lose her life whether she went in to the king or refused to go. The plot was for the universal slaughter of all Jews, so whether a queen or a servant, all alike were to be destroyed.

Secondly, it was made clear that her failure would not prevent deliverance being granted from some other quarter. In these words we see the strength of Mordecai's faith. If ever there was a point in this book when God's name should have occurred it is here, but that was not possible because of the nature of the record. However, in that great deliverance envisaged there would be no hope of her sharing, but she and her house would be destroyed. Thus, failing to do what she could do was such an evil that she would be punished for it. Thirdly, she was reminded that she was most likely put into the position where she was in a providential way, so as to be able to perform this special duty. Already we have stressed the forethought of God in having His instruments in place for all events. It is important to note here that Mordecai himself was fully confident of this principle, and brought home to Esther the deep secret of why she had been exalted to the highest position in the land, even though a Jew, a position which a woman of any other nation might well have filled. By pressing Esther into this crisis Mordecai may appear to have acted rather harshly with his cousin, the girl he loved from childhood, but she was never more dear to him than when he put this burden upon her. He spoke as one who had no doubt about the outcome, and as one who had traced the hand of God in the events of the past. Such firm words must have helped her to give her immortal reply, and strengthened her confidence at the time when she felt most timid.

ESTHER'S FINAL REPLY (4:15 - 17)

In spite of the risk involved and with the full knowledge of the consequences she faced if she were not accepted by the king, she sent word to her cousin and said, "I will go in unto the king". This promise was not lightly made, for she was quite young and had worn the golden crown for five years, but of what value would it be to her if she were not spared to wear it? We can well understand her request that there should be a gathering together of all the Jews who were at Shushan, and that unitedly they should fast for three days. This time of fasting would include not only those in the palace but also those in the city. Such deep exercise was judged by her to be vital preparation for her risky venture. This meeting of mourners is in sharp contrast to Esther's first meeting, when, with all the beautiful maidens, she had met to enjoy the special favours afforded to them and her. The three days fasting would in no way improve her appearance, but would be more likely to give her countenance a drawn and weary look. While prayer is not mentioned, being out of keeping with the tenor of this book, yet we may be sure that along with the fasting there would be earnest supplications ascending to God. The practice of fasting at a time of crisis seems to have been introduced in Judges 20 when the tribe of Benjamin, the one to which Esther belonged, was victorious over the Israelites for a time, but was later almost annihilated by them. It was fairly common in the days of the kings and also in the post-captivity period, so her request was not abnormal nor unique. At this time the Jews in Persia were being made to feel their need and, in the providence of God, were given a period sufficiently long to enable them to grasp the seriousness of their plight. All were compelled to appreciate that their lives depended upon the success of her acceptance and intercession. Just as in former times the nation had owed its survival to special individuals, so on this occasion those in captivity were made to realise their dependence upon one who formerly was but a humble maid. This fasting was a deep contrast to the feasting of Haman and the king, and to the long time of feasting with which the book is introduced.

Those who intercede must have at least two qualifications: firstly, they must have a love for those for whom they intercede; and secondly they must have access to the one with whom they intercede. Many in the empire had a deep love for the Jews, but they had no access to the king; some had access to the king but had no love for the distressed people. Esther had both of these, so she was fully fitted for the task she was called upon to do. The believer now has access to God and, with a love in his heart for those who are doomed to destruction, he can intercede in prayer for them and see them delivered from eternal death.

Esther volunteering to risk her life for the sake of her people reminds us of former deliverers who also did something similar. Moses, going in to the presence of Pharaoh and demanding the release of his people at the birth of the nation, is one that springs to mind. The courage he showed in facing a man who reckoned himself to be a god should never be underestimated. Likewise David's venturing to meet the giant with his sling and stones will ever be remembered as an outstanding act of bravery. Without thinking of herself as a heroine, or imagining that her name would go down in history as one of the deliverers of her people, Esther was prepared to go into the king's presence irrespective of what it might cost her to do so. She is the only woman in Scripture who was called upon to risk her life for her people.

Being a key figure in the purposes of God, and playing a vital role in His programme, may appeal to human ambition, but a look back over past history will show that in almost every case those involved in such important matters were brought to realise that their lives were at stake. The greatest deliverer of all, our Lord Jesus Christ, could say, "I lay down my life", and His servant Paul used the words, "neither count I my life dear unto myself". John tells us "we ought to lay down our lives for the brethren" (1 John 3:16). "The good shepherd giveth his life for the sheep" are words which are not only true of the Lord

Himself, but also of all shepherds who care for the saints. There must have been many in the empire who would have envied Esther her high position, but none of these would have liked to face the ordeal that she had to face. Many like a good position, but do their utmost to evade the responsibility that comes with it.

Of all the world empires referred to in Scripture none seemed to set so much store by law-keeping as that of the Medes and Persians. They not only gloried in the fact that what they decreed could not be altered, but also that it be obeyed without question. Haman took advantage of this, and stressed the point that the people he sought to destroy were characteristically disobedient to the laws of the land, so their destruction would be to the betterment of the empire. It is therefore worthy of note that Esther's venturing to enter the king's private quarters was "not according to law". She was in serious breach of the fixed etiquette of the palace. Only those invited could safely pass through those doors. What a contrast to our privilege now, for the most humble of the saints can enter the presence of "the King of kings", and do so with boldness. Where "law" is the order of the day, distance is associated with it, as was true of the old economy; but now that "grace" reigns, the message is, "Let us come boldly unto the throne of grace". May we make the best possible use of our privilege.

ESTHER ACCEPTED BY THE KING (5:1 - 2)

We come now to the great crisis of the story, for while much that we have been considering has been dramatic, nothing so far has been so vital as this approach to the king. Not only was the life of Esther at stake, but the survival of her people was also involved. Physically she could not have been feeling at her best, for the absence of food for so long must have shown in her countenance, and mentally she must have been in a tense state, especially as she knew the risk she was taking. However, the hour she most dreaded arrived; so after three days of deep distress and strict fasting, Esther, dressed in her royal robes, ventured to approach the king. Apparently, she entered the court and stood in a position where the king could see her, but did not draw near to him until she knew how she would be received. Unlike most monarchs, who sit on the throne only on state occasions, Ahasuerus occupied it when residing in the palace. The sight of the queen seeking an audience with him must have startled him, and made him conscious that something special was pressing her to act in this way. This explains the important question he put to her: "What is thy request?", and the outlandish offer he made to her of anything even to the half of his kingdom. His rashness and eccentric way of acting are manifest in this bold statement. Had she taken him at his word and asked for half of the kingdom, he likely would have turned down her request and told her it was one he could not fulfil. Herod, as recorded in the Gospels, made a similar offer to his daughter, but alas! he kept his promise, with the result John the Baptist lost his head. All her anxious anticipations and accumulated fears proved to be groundless, for no sooner did she appear than she found acceptance with him. If her heart had been struck with terror when she first was asked to intercede for her people, it must at this time not only have felt relief, but also have bounded with joy at the reception she was granted. The golden sceptre held out to her ended her dreads, and symbolised to her that all was well with her plan. Whether or not her hand trembled when she touched it we are not told, but we can be sure that never before nor after did anyone in Shushan appreciate being granted the favour more than she did that day. How different the story would have been if, instead of the sceptre greeting her, she had been charged with intrusion and slain by the sword. One stroke would have ended her beauty, and her blood would have drenched her royal garments. We might be tempted to think that the danger here stated was mere imagination, and that no one would ever be so cruelly treated by his fellow creature; but we must remember that life was cheap in the thoughts of kings, who viewed themselves as gods and their people as expendable material. The rod of authority, symbolised by the sceptre, appears to have been a feature of rulers in those days. Of later times, a sword was more common. One of the most difficult lessons for all of us to learn is, that what we dread most may never befall us: "The clouds we so much dread, are big with mercy and can break with blessings on our head". Esther may have said to herself, "What a fool was I to spend three days in distress, when all turned out as well as it did". However, we know it was God who turned the king's heart toward her, so the true facts were that her supplications and the cries of all the Jews found their response in the workings of His hand, though this be not acknowledged in this book. "The king's heart is in the hand of the Lord, as the rivers of water: he turneth it whithersoever he will" (Prov 21:1), is a statement exemplified on this occasion. Unknown to Ahasuerus or any of his courtiers, the acceptance of Esther was no mere natural response to her beauty, but rather to the overruling of a Master hand.

ESTHER INVITES THE KING AND HAMAN TO A BANQUET (5:3 - 8)

Before Esther had time to make known the purpose of her intrusion, the king detected she had some special request before her, and one which caused her to take this unusual step; so he called out, "What is thy request?" The word translated "request" here is exclusive to Esther except for Ezra 7:6. Later another synonymous word is used, "petition" (7:2). The distinction between these is slight: "request" implies seeking after something, and "petition" suggests asking for it. The question and promise left the door wide open for her to unburden her heart. To our surprise she did not immediately make her request, but rather deferred it, and instead, invited him and Haman to a banquet that very day. Her invitation was accepted, so Haman was summoned to share with the king the promised banquet. If with our mind's eye we look at the table, and view the three who are partaking together of the bounties thereon, we cannot help but be amazed. Haman, the murderer, like Judas in the upper-room, is having his last happy meal before his death. How Esther sat and ate with him without showing her resentment is difficult to imagine, but in her strategy she exhibits wisdom beyond our expectation.

Not until the next day would Esther disclose her request to the king. Again this is strange to our way of thinking. Mostly we seek to be rid of our burdens as soon as possible, and swiftly grasp every opportunity to do so. Obviously she was assured of the favour of the king, and knew there was nothing lost by her delay. "He that believeth shall not make haste" (Isa 28:16) could well be viewed as her text that day. However, her strange reluctance to explain her purpose in coming to him must have been perplexing, both to himself and Haman, and more especially when she was asked to do so a second time. It could well be that this bewilderment was the cause of his insomnia mentioned later in the book. What makes her delay more surprising is the fact that so many other matters in this book were done in haste. For example: the things that were given Esther were given speedily (2:9); the posts sent out with the decree of Haman were sent in haste (3:15); the king caused Haman to hasten to the banquet (5:5); the king ordered him to make haste and dress Mordecai (6:10); Haman hasted to his house mourning (6:12); he is hastened to attend the second banquet (6:14); and the king's commandment hastened the posts with the second decree (8:14). None of these occasions of hastening was more important than the answer to the king's request, yet it was deferred until the second banquet. Whether Esther herself rested during the night between these two banquets is impossible to say, but if she was like most of us she shared with the king a sleepless night.

Much concern must have filled the breasts of the Jews in Shushan during these two days. They would have learned that Esther had been accepted, but their main burden was to know whether her intercession on their behalf was successful. Waiting for news at a time of crisis is very trying, but God not only delivers His people, but often teaches them patience in doing it. "Though it tarry wait for it" (Hab 2:3) is not only a word to the prophet, but also a principle of God's dealings with His own. In a special way the future remnant will have to learn this, for their deliverance will appear to them to be long delayed. How precious to note that even the Lord Himself waited until "His hour" came. He knew what lay before Him, but He also knew that His Father had a programme and a timetable, so He willingly waited until the appointed time, and then gave Himself over to those who crucified Him. His enemies did not want to kill Him when they did, but God overruled their plans and "in due time Christ died for the ungodly".

HAMAN'S DELIGHT SPOILED BY MORDECAI
(5:9 - 14)

Those who climb to great heights are often troubled with dizziness. Haman cannot help feeling proud that he alone has been singled out to share in the banquet with the king and queen. He is elated with the prosperity which has befallen him and the honours heaped upon his head. However, once out of the palace and passing through the gate, he was confronted with this strange spectacle: a mere Jew refusing to show him the least respect, or to even rise from his seat as the prince passed through. The decree being enacted did not change Mordecai, nor did it cause him to alter his way of acting in order that it might be reversed. Had Haman's hand been as able as his heart was willing, the end of Mordecai was reached, but he passed on, and returned to his home to inform his family of his amazing prosperity.

A formal reunion of his near relatives was called at which he boasted of his wealth and of his sons, but very specially of the unique honour conferred upon him by being the sole one to be invited to share with the king and queen the important royal banquet due the next day. If ever a man was filled with earthly glory, he was that man. What more could he obtain except the throne itself? There must have been many selfish nobles surrounding the king; some of their names have already been mentioned in this book, but to the gratification of his proud heart he had eclipsed them all. Obviously his promotion had been rapid, and came as a surprise even to himself, as well as to others. Being the father of ten sons suggests that by this time he was not young, so he must have passed many years in obscurity before he flashed into the light of popularity. Many men are in high places, but all they have is an outward show, for quite often honours die with their possessor. Haman, however, had wealth as well as honour, and he viewed his sons as the heirs of his rich inheritance, and the men who would perpetuate his name for years to come. His boastful spirit reminds us of a greater than he,

Nebuchadnezzar, who expressed his pride and said, "Is not this great Babylon, that I have built for the house of the kingdom by the might of my power, and for the honour of my majesty?" (Dan 4:30). How different are the words of the King of kings, "I am meek and lowly in heart" (Matt 11:29).

In this passage we are given an insight into the vain heart of fallen man. All that is valuable in his eyes are his possessions, his sons and his promotion to earthly honour. The passing of time has not changed his ambitions, for to this day the same aims and ideas fill the minds of the ungodly. How different it is with the saints, "Whose nest hangs in no forest of all this death doomed land". Perhaps if we were as ambitious to possess our spiritual inheritance, as the worldlings are to possess theirs, we would be much wiser than we are.

Mordecai's refusal to bow was the fly in the ointment of Haman. The defiance of the Jew was too much for him to stomach, and almost demolished his sandcastle of pride. However his wife, Zeresh, was quick to propose a solution to his problem. Her idea was to have this offending fellow hanged on gallows fifty cubits high, and to do so as soon as possible. The sanction of the king had to be obtained for this execution, so it had to wait until he returned to the palace in the morning. With this detestable creature out of sight the banquet could be enjoyed without any distress or anger. His body dangling in the air would bring no distress to his executioners, but would mean that never again would he hurt the pride of Haman, or kill his joy. Her plan would mean the destruction of the ringleader of the Jewish resistance, and he would be the first sample of the ruin of the rest of his people which were to be executed at the end of the year. Many have wondered why the gallows were to be so high, but possibly the purpose was that the victim would be so elevated that all in Shushan would see in him a sample of their lot when the appointed day would come. In this part of the story we can trace faint pictures of past and future events. Had Mordecai been executed as designed by Zeresh, he would have been the first human type of Christ on the Cross. Just as Mordecai was expected to be hanged while Haman feasted at the banquet, so Christ was crucified at the time when the Jews were keeping the Passover feast. In a future day there will be a time of rejoicing when God's two witnesses will be killed and their bodies left unburied in the street of Jerusalem. The Antichrist and his supremo, like Haman, will have to endure the opposition of these two men for almost three and one half years, so when they will be removed all those in league with these evil rulers will celebrate the victory by sending presents to one another (Rev 11:7 - 10). One sombre feature of all these cases is that boasters no sooner reach the pinnacle of their pride than their fall ensues. It could well be that the faithful remnant in the future will receive much encouragement from the story of the book of Esther. Again we have another principle of Proverbs illustrated, "Pride goeth before destruction, and an haughty spirit before a fall" (16:18).

MORDECAI HONOURED (6:1 - 11)

These verses may appear to be parenthetical, for in a sense they interrupt the story, but they still have to do with Haman, who on this occasion is not filling the place of honour, but rather being compelled to honour the one man he bitterly hated. Such a reversal of fortunes could never have been brought about by human plans, but was the direct result of divine intervention. One of the most common ways God had used to intervene in the lives of kings was to disturb their sleep. The cases of Abimelech (Gen 20:3),

Pharaoh (Gen 41:1), and Nebuchadnezzar (Dan 2:1) are examples which readily come to mind. Even in the Book of Job we are reminded that "God speaketh ... in a dream, in a vision of the night" (33:14 - 15). However, on this occasion, His way was to disturb the king so much that his sleep went from him. In order to while away the time, and possibly to soothe his mind, he called for the book of the chronicles to be read to him. As we have already pointed out, these records were almost exclusively about the achievements of the king and the successes of his campaigns. Little is said in them of the disasters which oftentimes befell the armies of the empire. Such reading, like a story at bedtime sometimes read to children, was expected to calm his mind and end his insomnia. In the course of the reading, the record concerning the preservation of the life of the king through the intervention of Mordecai was rehearsed. Upon hearing of this important feat of honour, the question arose in the king's mind as to whether or not this special act of devoted loyalty had been suitably rewarded. On hearing that it had been passed over and that no recognition had been given Mordecai for his timely and vitally important action, the king was greatly stirred, for at length it dawned upon him that he owed his life to this man who lived an obscure life and was deemed to be so unimportant in the empire. In a trice he decided to rectify the matter and, even though belatedly, afford Mordecai the honour due to him and the renown he had earlier earned. The sovereignty of God can be seen in all this, for He so arranged the events as to have His representative honoured at the very time he was in distress, and by the very man who had planned his murder. But for Mordecai's loyalty someone else would have been the king of Persia, and the least Ahasuerus should have done in return was to give him some public recognition for his honourable action. With all the excitement which no doubt had occurred at Shushan at the time when the king was almost killed by two of his trusted servants, the great concern for his safety would have helped to eclipse any thought of rewarding the man who had informed the court of his danger. At almost the conclusion of the reading, and early in the morning, Haman returned from his home to attend the palace. He had one special request to bring to the king, and it alone filled his thoughts; it was to obtain from him permission to hang Mordecai on the prepared gallows. Apparently he had no dread of coming before the king, but almost as soon as he entered the court and was identified, he was given an audience. The question on the king's lips, "What shall be done unto the man whom the king delighteth to honour?" fell upon Haman's ears as sweet music, for after all the favours shown him by the king in the recent past, he concluded that still more honours were coming his way. He could think of no person in the entire realm other than himself who could be more closely associated with king. Full well he knew that he was the apple of the king's eye, for rising almost daily from one position of honour to another, even to the rank of being the only one chosen to attend the queen's private banquet, left him in no doubt that the person to be so distinctly honoured could be none other than himself.

In giving the answer to the king's question, Haman, thinking only of himself, went as far as possible in asking for all that marked the ruling monarch. Here in this book we are allowed yet another insight into the human heart. The Evil One, who said, "I will be like the most High", puts into the hearts of his dupes the same spirit of pride as fills his own being. If we look at the fivefold answer to the king's question, we cannot help asking, "What more could he have added to the list that would have made the one being honoured more like the king?" When the people of the city would see the spectacle riding past with all these adornments, they would scarcely distinguish him from the sovereign. His royal robe, that is one already worn by the king; the horse normally ridden by him, with a crown on its head (though disputed by some, it appears from the original that the crown here referred to was not put on Mordecai but on the horse); the most honoured servant leading the horse; and the proclamation, all combine to make the display one of majestic glory. At the time when Haman was speaking these things his heart must have been swelling with pride and excitement. Indeed, he must have imagined that the greatest day in his life had arrived. However, to his astonishment and horror he was ordered to do these very things to Mordecai, the man he most hated. The day he had anticipated would be the greatest day of his life had suddenly become the most distressing. When the balloon of pride bursts then all falls flat and the display is over. In Mordecai's case, his darkest days were before the dawn of his glory, but in Haman's case his brightest days were before his fall.

There was nothing Haman could do but obey the king's command, so the decree was executed, albeit reluctantly. Perhaps it was the first time Mordecai had sat on a horse, just as it was the only time he ever wore royal garments. This apparel was strikingly different from the rent garments and sackcloth worn by him when he learned of the plot of Haman (4:1). The man who refused to stand up and reverence the prince, was lifted up and treated with dignity by the one who demanded, but failed to obtain, his respect. The exaltation of Mordecai sounded the death knell for Haman; from now on it would be degradation not elevation for him. Even his wife, as we shall see, was wise enough to grasp this. If we visualise the sight of a humble Jew being led with royal honours through the city by his most avowed enemy, we cannot help seeing the shadow of a far greater event when the One who was once despised and rejected will ride in triumph, not through Shushan, but into Jerusalem (Rev 19:11 - 13). Even the past history of the Jews had shown examples not unlike what is here. Whether we think of Joseph riding in Pharaoh's chariot, and the cry before him, "Bow the knee" (Gen 41:43), or of Solomon riding on David's mule (1 Kings 1:33), we can see a foreshadowing of the future glory of the King of kings. When the parade was over, Mordecai returned to the king's gate, so he was not elated by his experience but retained his previous concern for his life and the life of his people. The dangers awaiting him had not been averted by his temporary honour. News from the queen that she had succeeded in nullifying the evil plot would have meant more to him than a ride on the king's horse. On the other hand, this exaltation and honour may have encouraged him by giving him a token of what was about to happen in the king's court.

From these few verses that we are considering we can learn several lessons. One of these is the suddenness of the changes that can be experienced. One day made great changes in the lives of two men. Haman rose in the morning with well-prepared plans to execute Mordecai by hanging him high on the gallows; but instead, probably before noon, he had to lead through the streets of the city, lifted up on horseback, the very one he detested, and with his own mouth proclaim, "This is the man whom the king delighteth to honour". The morning of the same day found Mordecai sad and despondent at the thought of the threatened destruction of himself and his people. But to his surprise, and to the surprise of many about him, he found himself being dressed, not in sackcloth as before, but in the king's robe, and instead of sitting in humility at the king's gate, sitting on the horse the king had ridden. Something of the Lord's doings in this way was in the mind of Hannah when she said, "He bringeth low, and lifteth up. He raiseth up the poor out of the dust, and lifteth up the beggar from the dunghill" (1 Sam 2:7 - 8). Another obvious lesson these verses teach is that God allows His enemies to reach the point when they imagine their aims have been achieved, but just at the time when they are most confident He blows upon their whole scheme. Whether we think of Pharaoh pursuing the fleeing Israelites, or of the greatest of all examples of this principle, the crucifixion of Christ, the whole evil plan was defeated in each case· by the destruction of Pharaoh and his hosts in the former, and by the resurrection of Christ in the latter. A third lesson taught in these verses is that such wonders are wrought by God in places where we would least expect to see them. In Persia the name of God was almost unheard of, yet even there He sat supreme and controlled all that was transpiring. The men in authority thought they were ordering everything, and expected to fulfil all their purposes, yet in the end they witnessed their whole scheme being shattered, and that in ways of which they had never thought. Had we watched the men erecting the gallows we might have concluded that God was taking no notice of what was being done, and that evil was on the throne while righteousness was in the dust. But only a few hours would pass before such groundless thoughts were proven to be totally vain. We may not always know where God draws the line beyond which He will not allow His enemies to pass, but we can be assured that such a line exists.

HAMAN RETURNS TO HIS HOME (6:12 - 14)

Like most men in trouble, Haman returned to his house to seek comfort from his loved ones. In ch 5:10 he is said to have arrived at the same house full of jubilation, and elated that he had been invited to the banquet prepared by Esther. This time all was different. His head covered with grief, he rushed in to tell his wife and all his friends the strange and sad happenings of the morning. To his surprise, instead of hearing consoling words from her, she confirmed his worst fears by predicting the certainty of his fall. This humiliation was a token of the ruin which was sure to follow because the man involved was of "the seed of the Jews". No doubt such words left him in despair. She was absolutely sure that there was something supernatural about the Jewish people. What had transpired convinced her that the tide had turned, and that her husband was on the slippery slope to ruin. At the end of ch. 5 she had given him instructions as to how he could dispose of Mordecai, but now she was convinced that no force could resist him or his people. This brief call by her husband turned her world upside down and left the home, which a few hours before had been a scene of happiness, a place of bewilderment and distress. Little did she know when he left her to attend the banquet that she would never see him alive again. Like the mother of Sisera, looking in vain to see her son return from the battle with goodly spoils, while, unknown to her, he was already dead in the tent with a peg driven through his head (Jud 5:28 - 30), so Zeresh was to be disappointed with the outcome of the banquet.

THE SECOND BANQUET AND ITS OUTCOME (7:1 - 10)

At length the momentous hour arrived when the king, the queen and Haman sat down together to share the feast prepared. For the third time the vital question was put to Esther, "What is thy petition, queen Esther? and it shall be granted thee; and what is thy request? and it shall be performed". While the offer was twofold, in a sense the request was essentially one. She could delay no longer, so duly the promised answer was given. In plain and pointed words she unburdened her heart and made plain to the king that what concerned her was a matter of life or death. She and her people had been sentenced to destruction, and were awaiting the day of their execution. Had slavery been allotted to them, she would have accepted it without troubling the king or seeking his intervention, but the wiping out of her entire nation was more than she could endure in silence. Even enslavement would have been damaging to the king, for it would have put out of useful service an industrious and trustworthy people. The next great question which rose in the king's mind was, "Who is he, and where is he, that durst presume in his heart to do so?" Without hesitation she named Haman as the culprit. The shock was so great that the king left the table and went into the fresh air to allow his mind to settle, and to give time for him to decide what to do. In his absence Haman tried to plead with Esther in the hope that she would intercede with the angry king, and obtain from him some mercy for her avowed enemy. At first he stood to plead, but in his desperation he fell down and held her in some way. Returning at that moment to the banquet hall, the king's wrath was intensified at seeing his servant acting with such a lack of decorum toward her majesty. In the sovereignty of God, one of the most honourable chamberlains was present and related to the king what he knew of the plans of Haman regarding the gallows, in a way which must have weighed heavily with the king, for he reminded him that the man for whom the gibbet was prepared had spoken good concerning him. The die was cast, and Haman's sentence pronounced. The king said, "Hang him thereon". We must remember that these gallows were erected in the precincts of Haman's house, so all that was befalling him would have been visible to his wife and family. Had her plans succeeded Mordecai would have been hanged, but how sad must have been the family circle when the one they all admired, and to whom they owed so much, was hanged at their own door.

A number of valuable lessons can be learned from this part of the story. To begin with, it demonstrates how quickly matters can change, alike for those who know God and for those who are strangers to Him. In a matter of hours the fears of Esther were dispelled, and in a much shorter time the fame of Haman was shattered. Her original dread of entering uninvited into the king's presence had abated somewhat by this time, but the black cloud of the threatened execution of herself and her people still remained over her head. Her supreme objective in entertaining the king was to obtain deliverance from the wicked decree of Haman. She took her own time to plead her case, and when the right moment arrived she frankly stated it, but did so in a most tactful manner.

If we think of her intercession for her life and people in the presence of the king, we could derive some help in our exercise before God regarding the need of the perishing. Not that we need have any dread in approaching Him, for we are encouraged to "come boldly unto the throne of grace", but how often our requests for our fellow-men are expressed without realising the seriousness of what is involved in their doom should they die unsaved. Even in prayer meetings prior to the preaching of the gospel it is not uncommon to hear men praying without any trace of feeling for the deep need of the lost. In some cases, were the one praying to have his eyes open we would conclude he was preaching to men rather than pleading with God. No one listening to Esther would have been in any doubt about the seriousness of her plight. Just as she was the one privileged to speak to the king, and was alone able to intercede with him, so we are those who can come to the throne and are responsible to do so. Her people needed her to plead with the king, and the perishing world needs us to plead with God for it. However, there is this great difference: Esther's people were of little value to Ahasuerus, but the world of sinners is loved by God.

A further lesson is here, for we can see that when faced with this sudden dilemma the king did not act with his usual rashness, but immediately resorted to a solitary place for a time. Quick reaction can be dangerous in such cases, for many have done something on the spur of the moment which later they regretted. A little reflection and serious thought can save us from many blunders.

This banquet-table in Shushan furnishes us with another shadow of things more familiar to us. In an upper room in Jerusalem there was another table, a table at which the King was seated in the presence of a deceitful foe. Just as Haman was exposed at the banquet, so Judas was exposed at the supper table, and just as Haman was taken from the banquet and hanged, so Judas went out and hanged himself. Again, there are distinct differences between the two stories, for all was a surprise to Ahasuerus, but not so to the Lord. Likewise the evil of Judas was a surprise to the apostles, but the evil of Haman was no surprise to Esther.

This execution of Haman is an example of what is commonly called "poetic justice" or, as Scripture expresses it, of one "reaping" what he has "sown". All in Shushan who knew of Haman's plot, and most of them did, expected to see Mordecai hanging from the lofty gallows in the precincts of Haman's house, but to their surprise they beheld the plotter himself pilloried on it.

THE KING'S DECREE ON BEHALF OF THE JEWS
(ch. 8:1 - 17)

ESTHER GIVEN HAMAN'S ESTATE (8:1 - 2)

Seldom in any empire have so many dramatic changes taken place in so short a time, as those which occurred at the palace of Shushan on that memorable day. It began with Haman rushing to attend the banquet, and ended with his dead body dangling from a gallows in his yard. It began with Mordecai full of sorrow and dread, and ended with him raised to the post of prime minister. It began with Esther venturing to plead for her people and expose the enemy's plot, and ended with her people being spared and her cousin being welcomed into the king's presence. Mordecai was not the first Jew to be lifted from lowliness to honour, for as we have already seen Joseph was taken from prison to become the prime minister of Egypt. Both he and Mordecai were exalted in the absence of their brethren. Likely none in Jerusalem knew anything of the deliverance of their brethren in captivity, nor did Joseph's brethren know that their rejected brother was exalted to lofty heights in the land where he was sold for a slave. The world may despise the "Man of sorrows", but time will show that God has not only exalted Him to His own right hand, but will exalt Him on earth, the scene of His sorrows.

Until this banquet, Ahasuerus knew nothing of the relationship between the queen and Mordecai. Indeed, the fact that both were Jews was also kept hidden from him. "Esther had not yet showed her kindred nor her people" (2:20) are words which show us that at the time of her marriage the king was not careful to ascertain the nationality of his new bride. So long as she pleased him and satisfied the requirements of his mind, it apparently mattered nothing to him from which race she came. However, from this day forward he knew he had not only a Jew for his queen, but also one on his inner council.

There were two significant offers made by the king to Mordecai. One concerned the management of Haman's estate, the other the ring taken from him before he was hanged. In keeping with his exaltation to the position of prime minister, he must reside in a suitable mansion. There is no record of where he lived while sitting daily in the king's gate, but it may well be that he slept in one of the corridors of the guard lodges usually found at royal palaces. However all that was at an end, for from henceforth he would live in the mansion formerly occupied by Haman. Never in all his life had this poor Jew been so wealthy. We may be sure that Haman feathered his nest with all that he could muster of the treasures of the empire, and that his house was in keeping with his high position. Little did he think when he was gathering these precious things and building his mansion that they would all be enjoyed by the despised man whom he hated. Mordecai would have been happy to remain a poor Jew so long as his life was spared, but this would not satisfy the king. We too, who have experienced deliverance from our threatened doom, would have been thankful for ever had this been all that was done for us, but God, like the king, has enriched us with spiritual blessings and seated us, not in earthly glory, but in heavenly places in Christ, so that we can sing, "Not only snatched from burning hell, but to God's bosom brought".

Poor Haman, like most worldlings, failed to realise the uncertainty of his riches. He was not only taken away from them, but none of them were left to his family. His wife, who planned the execution of Mordecai, like her partner was totally ignorant of the ways of the God of the Jews. She could see nothing in those people but a detestable race, with laws contrary to all other peoples, a people the world would be better without. Many have seriously thought that what Mordecai and his people were called to pass through was the punishment they deserved for not embracing the opportunity of returning to their own land when Cyrus opened the door for their release. What does surprise most is that God not only worked for the good of the returned captives, but also for those who failed to return. However heavily He may smite His wayward children, yet He never fails them when they are in need, and however severe may be His treatment of the nation which turned to idolatry, yet it is "beloved for the fathers' sakes" (Rom 11:28). Again, we can trace the hand of God in all the happenings at Shushan, yet, due to the nature of this book, there is no mention of Him in the story.

The signet ring taken from Haman and given to Mordecai may not appear to be of great significance to us, but it was more than a mere ornament for his finger. Anyone possessing it could stamp with authority any document, and then it carried the same weight as if the king himself had stamped it. Instead of the normal signature in writing, the impression of this ring in the soft wax turned any document into a royal decree.

This part of the story reminds us of the crises which do arise in the lives of the saints. They may not be a matter of life and death, but God arranges our affairs so that we are brought to feel our helplessness and our utter dependence upon Himself. Indeed, our conversion experience is a kind of pattern of His dealings in after life. It will be remembered that it was just when we were most despairing that the light shone into our hearts. Again we can see that in our experiences, God not only delivers, but goes far beyond our expectations in lavishing blessings upon us.

THE REVERSAL OF HAMAN'S DECREE (8:3 - 14)

While the generous treatment of the king had relieved both Esther and Mordecai of all anxiety regarding their own lives, it had not altered the fate of the Jews throughout the empire. However pathetically Esther pled with the king, and on this second appeal she wept as she did so, yet he was in a difficulty. For though he was keen to deliver the Jews and remove from them the threat, yet according to Persian law he could not reverse the decree of Haman, for it was sealed with the king's ring. Esther assumed that he had the power to do what she asked, but it was not in his hand to accede to her request. No document written in the king's name and sealed with his ring could be revoked. There was, however, a way out of the dilemma, and resort was made to it. A new decree could be published with the same authority as the original one, and this could be so worded as to nullify the effects of the former one. Mordecai was given the task of composing this important document, and of making sure it reached every corner of the empire. As happened when Haman's decree was despatched, great care was exercised to make sure that, when copies of the decree would reach the different countries, it was written in the various languages suited to each, so that all in them might understand its content. When we think of the extent of the vast empire we are made conscious of the amount of travelling involved in the reaching of its remotest bounds, especially in days when riding on domesticated animals was the fastest way of transport. These animals were in all probability selected to suit the terrain over which they had to travel. The camels and dromedaries would traverse the deserts, and the horses and mules could be employed on the highways. The absence of asses in this list is notable, but the mules may have displaced them.

The new decree gave the Jews the right to defend themselves against all attackers who would seek their hurt. Some have blamed them for their cruelty in slaying so many, but those slain were those who attempted to take advantage of the first decree, and who had been waiting for the day to arrive when they could become rich, in a matter of hours, at the expense of the Jews. The details of this decree are clearly set forth, so that there could be no misunderstanding of them. The threatened people were to assemble together, and so assist one another as well as show their unity. They were to stand for their lives, so it was not a case of unprovoked attack on their neighbours but rather a defensive war to preserve their lives. All their assailants were to be slain and destroyed, including the children and women. Just as the decree of Haman was devised to strip the Jews of their wealth, so this one gave authority to the Jews to take the spoil of their enemies. (However, as we shall see later, they did not claim their rights, but left the spoil to those who were spared). The experience of Mordecai on the day of Esther's second banquet was a preview of what his people would enjoy on the thirteenth day of the twelfth month. The relief from anxiety and grief, and the honours bestowed upon him were not to be limited to him personally, but were to be shared by his entire people. Thus the man who brought them into this critical distress was the man who was instrumental in their enrichment.

As we have already pointed out, and those acquainted with prophecy will have no difficulty in conceding it, this story is a shadow of the great tribulation, or the time of Jacob's trouble. At that time, just when all hope for the survival of the nation of Israel will be at an end, the Lord will come to her relief, riding on His white horse, and thus will quickly bring to an end all her sorrow. Again, as the execution of the second decree resulted in the destruction of the Jews' enemies, so His coming will be "in flaming fire taking vengeance on them that know not God" (2 Thess 1:8). The nation was born in sorrow in Egypt, and its rebirth will be preceded by even greater sorrows. The spoil from those who will surround Jerusalem in that day will be very great, and will provide the city and the nation with all the wealth that will be required to establish the coming kingdom.

There is an unchanging principle in the dealings of God with His enemies. It is this: those who hurt His people not only suffer His wrath, but also have their wealth taken from them and given to those they persecuted. However, in this case, as in the case of Abraham defeating the kings in Gen 14, they did not accept the spoil even though they had the right to do so. Mordecai himself took the estate of Haman which was granted to him by the king, but later the people refused to take the spoil (9:10). At the deliverance from Egypt Israel spoiled the Egyptians and obtained from them some of the wages due for the years of slavery. This spoil was used to erect the tabernacle in the wilderness. The passing of centuries has not altered that divine principle, for here in the Book of Esther just as the curtain of the OT drops on the history of the Jews, it is seen to be still in operation, and that even where we would least expect to find it.

MORDECAI AND HIS PEOPLE REJOICE (8:15 - 17)

The closing three verses of this chapter give us one of the most delightful scenes of this book. Our imagination is stretched to its limit trying to visualise the man Mordecai being introduced to the king by his cousin. He entered the palace plainly dressed and possibly somewhat apprehensive and fearful as to what was in store for him, but left the king's presence dressed in royal apparel of blue and white, and carrying on his head a great crown of gold. Whatever ambiguity there may be in ch. 6:8 as to whether he or the horse on which he rode wore the crown, there is no doubt in this passage that it was he himself who was so adorned. The head that a few hours before was bowed in grief, is now held high in honour. Can we imagine the consternation of the people of the city and palace when their eyes fell upon the amazing sight? As we would expect, the reaction of the Jews, who were primarily involved in the struggle, was one of great joy and gladness. All had been darkness, but now all was light; all had been weeping and grief, but now all was rejoicing; and all had been shame and distress, but now all was honour. Their elation, just as their anguish, had its effect upon the city. In the former case we read, "the city Shushan was perplexed", but here, "the city Shushan rejoiced and was glad". Wherever the news spread throughout the empire the same results followed, so rejoicing and feasting became the order of the day. Moreover, the change in the fortunes of the Jews attracted some Gentiles to become Jews. They began to fear a people who had their fortunes so quickly reversed. While there is no mention of the power which wrought this miracle, yet we know it was the God of the Jews who had done so. Just as Ruth the Moabitess returned with Naomi and was absorbed into Israel at the time when "God had visited his people by giving them bread", so on this occasion the deliverance granted by God led some to see in Him One worthy to be trusted.

In the day when the Lord returns, who was once viewed as a despised Jew, His head will be crowned with many diadems, and with the sword of His mouth He will destroy all His own foes and those of the Jews. Then too, there will be rejoicing of the faithful. The nation which once looked on Him hanging on a tree will then see the same One in all His majesty and beauty.

Prophecy makes plain that in the day of Israel's restoration some will "take hold of the skirt of him that is a Jew, saying, We will go with you; for we have heard that God is with you" (Zec 8:23). God's presence with His people, and His power operating for them, has a profound effect upon those who are strangers to Him. The importance of His presence and power being manifest amongst His people in this age cannot be over-stressed. The vital difference between the gospel preached in divine power and mere lectures on theology is that the former produces results in the hearers, whereas the latter merely informs the mind. According to 1 Cor 14 if a stranger visits an assembly and witnesses the Lord's leading in the exercise of spiritual gift he will go out and "report that God is in you of a truth" (v. 25). We need more than a profession that His presence is with us, as promised in Matt 18:20; we must have some evidence of it.

THE JEWS DESTROY THEIR ENEMIES
(ch. 9:1 - 16)

TRIUMPH OF THE JEWS (9:1 - 16)

At length the great day which Haman had chosen by lot approached. The entire empire had waited for months for its arrival, for it was to change the portion of all who were in any sense connected to the Jewish people. At the hearing of the first decree, their enemies were full of expectation that when this thirteenth day of the twelfth month would arrive the land would be flooded with Jewish blood, and that they would be filling their houses with great spoil. Every day would be counted by them, for anxious as they were to take vengeance on these people whose laws were so diverse from their own, they had no option but to wait for the fixed date to come round. With the second and equally authorised decree also in circulation, many must have been confused as to exactly what would happen on the fatal day. Whatever effect the second decree had upon the people who learned of it, there was one thing sure: it in no way removed the enmity in the hearts of the enemies of the Jews. Some may have been less daring because of it, while others may have remained neutral, but when the test came, the number of enemies who attempted to destroy the Jews was substantial. We might well question whether the captives in the Persian Empire had any power to defend themselves, or had any equipment with which to do so. However, it is clear that they were not left to their own resources in this matter, for the rulers and all those in authority came to their help. This was due to the influence of Mordecai, whose fame at this time had penetrated to the remotest part of the empire. The narrative at this stage is constantly stressing the greatness of this new prime minister. At least five times we read of his greatness, so his exaltation was no mere flash in the pan but remained permanent.

We cannot but be surprised at the number, even in Shushan, who were opposed to the Jews. On the first day, some five hundred manifested their hatred of them and were slain by the sword. Amongst these were the ten sons of Haman, who were slain and afterwards hanged as their father had been. Their names are given, all ten of them, so he was left with neither root nor branch. Instead of the Jews being annihilated as he had planned, his whole household was wiped out. In all probability these sons shared his hatred as well as his riches, and so righteously deserved to share his doom. Those acquainted with ancient languages are agreed that each of them bore a Persian name, so this adds support to the view that he was not a descendant of Amalek, nor was he linked with Agag as some have imagined. On the fourteenth day more enemies were destroyed, and this increased the number slain at Shushan to eight hundred. Whatever else the wicked plot of Haman did at that time, one of its results was the bringing to light of those who hated the Jews. In a city like Shushan some Jews may not have known who were their friends and who were their foes, but when this crisis was over all was perfectly clear, for all were manifested in their true colours.

While the destruction of the Jews' enemies was going on at Shushan, the rest of the empire was likewise plunged into bloodshed. Apparently the enemy had assembled at different points to carry out the first decree on the day appointed, and likewise the Jews, in view of the second decree, assembled together to defend themselves, so a sort of civil war broke out. There is no mention of casualties from the Jewish ranks, but the number of their enemies slain (seventy five thousand) was surprisingly high. Even if we take the smaller number of the LXX (fifteen thousand), it is still much larger than we might expect. What these figures make plain is that there were many enemies of the Jews, and that the hatred of Haman's heart was shared by many throughout the empire. Sometimes God allows circumstances to arise which bring to the surface the inner feelings of men. Possibly the Jews never thought they were so much hated until this vital day. In a future time, the mark of the beast will brand all who are associated with him, and test to the full the reality of the faithful. Those who supported Haman in Persia shared his fate, and those who will take sides with the beast will have to share his doom, and go with him into the lake of fire.

Surprising enough is the statement, which occurs three times in the story, "On the spoil laid they not their hands". It was theirs for the taking, but they refused to exercise their rights. One likely reason for this was to prove that the slaughter of their enemies was not done to enrich themselves, but rather to save their lives. The only spoil that was confiscated was that which belonged to Haman and given to Mordecai. The Gentile population set great store on the spoils of their enemies, but the Jews were more enlightened and valued life more than goods. The Lord Himself stressed this in the well known words, "What shall it profit a man if he gain the whole world, and loose his own soul (or life)?". As far back as the days of Abram the same principle obtained when the king of Sodom said, "Give me the persons, and take the goods to thyself". The reply of Abram was, "I will not take from a thread even to a shoe latchet" (Gen 14:21 - 23). With so many thousands slain, the spoils must have been immense, but in spite of the comparative poverty of the Jews they were not prepared to become rich at the expense of their enemies. This high standard of principle manifest at this time is somewhat surprising, for after a century in heathen surroundings we would have expected the Jews to have drifted so far from God as to think as did those about them. Mordecai was not the only Jew in Persia who feared the Lord and viewed matters in a way that few, even in Jerusalem, viewed them. There may also have been an additional reason for letting go the spoil. Much of it may have been associated with idolatry. To bring into the home of a Jew that which would ruin both himself and his family would have been too costly in its results.

We still live in a world that sets a high value on material things, but the believer has his hopes in another world, and can say, "I count all things but loss for the excellency of the knowledge of Christ Jesus my Lord" (Phil 3:8). To him the salvation of souls is vastly more important than accumulating worldly wealth. The former will exist forever, while the latter endures only for time. Much grace and help from God are needed to enable him to refuse what is of the world, and what might cause his heart to drift away from Him, or even to feel in some respects no longer dependent upon His provision. It has ever been the will of God that His own should hold lightly all that the world has to offer. When Abram refused the spoils he was almost immediately assured by the words of the Lord, "Fear not, Abram, I am thy shield, and thy exceeding great reward" (Gen 15:1).

THE FEAST OF PURIM
(ch. 9:17 - 32)

THE CELEBRATION OF VICTORY (9:17 - 32)

The deliverance was so great an event in the thinking of Mordecai that he felt it was not only a time for rejoicing, but something that should never be forgotten by the Jews. He considered that just as the deliverance from Egypt was commemorated by the annual passover, so this latter deliverance should likewise be commemorated. Because of the extent of the empire and the amount of opposition the Jews encountered, all the destruction of the enemy could not be accomplished in one day, so the conflict extended into a second one. Some were rejoicing on the 14th day and others did not enjoy their victory until the 15th, so in order that all should rejoice together the celebrating feast lasted for two days. Thus both the 14th and the 15th became special days in the calendar of the Jews. There appears to be nothing religious about these days, but they were days of social pleasure, of relaxation, and for sending presents to friends. What does surprise us about them is the fact that they were, and still are, kept by the Jews in their own land. We could understand a feast established in Jerusalem being kept by some who were in captivity, but that a deliverance wrought for them in a Gentile environment, and far removed from their own land, should be celebrated by the returned remnant is amazing. It tells us that there was an appreciation of the oneness of the nation, so that what befell one part was viewed as though all were involved.

If history can be relied upon, the feast of Purim was continually kept by the nation even until NT times, so what it commemorated was no fleeting event, but one which impressed itself firmly upon the minds of the succeeding generations. It is not mentioned in either the Gospels or the Epistles, though some have suggested that it is the unnamed feast of John 5, but that is most unlikely. Not being a religious feast, nor one given by divine decree, we can be almost certain that it is ignored by all the writers of the NT. Most likely the Jews in captivity did not keep the Passover nor any other of the divinely ordained feasts, so in this new one they had a shadow of their former deliverance, and something to look forward to every year. That captives in a foreign land could have such joyful times, and forget for two days in each year their bondage and misery, is truly surprising. Although no appreciation of God is expressed in the book, yet we can see His tender hand in relieving the hard lot of His people, even though they were far from Him. At the very time when the returned captives were rejoicing in Jerusalem over the building of the Temple, the Jews who were absent and dwelling in a strange land were also rejoicing, but not in the building for divine worship, but in their deliverance from death.

The book of Esther begins with a great feast which lasted for six months, but it ends with one which continued to be kept for centuries. The name given to it, Purim (which means "lots"), was a constant reminder of the lots which were cast by Haman in order to find the right day to execute his evil design. Likewise it also recalled how the threatened disaster was turned to victory. Had it succeeded, the entire Jewish race in the vast empire of Persia would have been wiped out.

The closing part of this chapter reiterates much that has been said already, but the main emphasis is that the feast had royal sanction, and that it was not something devised by Mordecai personally. A second letter confirming the decree was despatched, and it gave detailed instructions as to how the feast was to be kept. Unlike the letter sent by Haman, this one contained "words of peace and truth", so it confirmed their confidence and banished their fears. There is a hint that the two days of feasting were to be preceded by a day of fasting. The idea behind this was to recall the time of fasting by Esther and her staff prior to her venturing into the king's presence.

There are important lessons in this part of the book which must not be missed. One of these is that God in His sovereignty sometimes allows circumstances to arise in order to bring to the surface the evil in men's hearts. When we learn of the thousands who were slain throughout the empire, we have to remember that these were all united against the Jews. Possibly, few of these were suspected as being to any great extent hostile to the captives who dwelt amongst them, but the door that Haman opened allowed them to come out in their true colours. Even during the life of Christ we would not have detected the full measure of hatred toward Him in the hearts of men until His crucifixion. The cross manifested fully the extent of His rejection. How so many could join in His condemnation, especially after the years of His tender ministry, is difficult to perceive. In a lesser degree, but with the same result, there can arise similar circumstances in the lives of the saints of the present age. When an opening is given for the world to show its hatred of them, without fail it brings to light the true feeling of the hearts of men. When the day of Haman's decree was over, all knew whose side their neighbours were on. Those who rose up to destroy the Jews little thought that they were out of harmony with the royal palace. When Haman sent his cruel message it had royal sanction, but all had changed at the palace, so they were acting out of step. Had they taken seriously the second decree from the king, they would have kept their hands off the Jews, and saved their own lives. In our case, however, we have not merely to keep in harmony with an earthly monarch, but with the King of kings. The disciples who were calling down fire were out of touch with the feelings of their Master, and had to be rebuked by Him. Quite often we fail to ask, "What does the Lord think of this situation?" If we can discern His mind then it is our duty to act according to His will. When some evil has been done to us, we must remember that God has said, "Vengeance belongeth unto me"; likewise when the friendship of the world would allure us we must remember that it is at enmity with God. We must not assume that the rejoicing at this feast was over the slaughter of the enemies, but rather was it due to their lives being spared.

THE GREATNESS OF MORDECAI
(ch. 10:1 - 3)

The short chapter which ends the book tells us of the state of the empire when this episode concerning the Jews was over. Ahasuerus had suffered severe losses at the hands of the Greeks, so was likely in great need of money to replace some of these, and also to pay the army which had failed to rise to his expectations. The king, who before the great campaign had feasted his govenors, was now in need of the wealth of all the states of his empire, so he imposed a tribute, not only upon the mainland but also upon the islands of the sea. This could go some way in strengthening his hand, should he need to go to battle again. Unlike some other tributes this one was not levied on strangers only, but upon the entire population. In keeping with all the records stored in the archives, the might and power of Ahasuerus was duly mentioned but without a hint of his sad defeat in Europe. Apparently it would be totally unacceptable for any disasters to be mentioned in such memoirs.

To our surprise the greatness of Mordecai is coupled with that of the king. Especially stressed is the fact that he was advanced to his important post by the king, for he had learned to value the once despised Jew, and had made him second in power in his kingdom. Thus the second world empire ended as did the first, with a Jew as near as possible to the chief ruler. It will be recalled that at the fall of Babylon, Daniel was made the third ruler of the kingdom (Dan 5:29). However, Mordecai was in a special way valued by his own people, the Jews. His interest in them was manifest as he sought their good, and spoke peace to them.

The mention of his seed might suggest to us that he had children, but that is not the idea in the word; rather it is a reference to his race or nation. Some suggest that he spoke up for the Jews, but the simplest idea is that as long as he was spared, his people were in peace.

The curtain of our story drops without taking us further into the experiences of the Jews in Persia, but with the happy assurance that one of their heaviest trials ended with glory heaped upon them. One of their number was established as queen, and another exalted to the position of prime minister.

This third reference to the "book of the chronicles of the kings of Media and Persia", given at almost the close of the book, reminds us again that we have not been reading a story of events written in a general way, but rather an official account of one special crisis in the kingdom; which explained why the Jews came to be so influential in the reign of Ahasuerus. Such an important matter was judged to be suited for preservation in the archives of the empire. This helps us to understand why there are no references to religious exercises in it, and why it is silent regarding God or idols. Probably neither before nor after was such a record placed therein. The silent testimony to the superiority of the Jew even in a place where none would expect to find it, is but a hint that the day will come when One who was viewed as a despised Jew will, like Mordecai, bring deliverance to His people and will establish them in undisturbable peace.

APPENDIX A

SUMMARY OF THE MAJOR LESSONS TAUGHT IN THIS BOOK

One of these lies upon its surface. It is that God has a deep interest in His earthly people, even though they may be far away from Him. "The gifts and calling of God are without repentance" is not only a truth taught in the NT, but one which covers the entire course of history. There were times when He was angry with their ways and chastised them, but if the enemy goes beyond being a mere instrument to carry out His chastening, then He will take strong dealings with such offences. The book of Isaiah makes plain that He uses the nations as a rod to punish His people for their sins, yet if those whom He commissions imagine that they are being helped by their gods, and act in selfish pride, then He will turn and deal with them to their destruction (Isa 10:3 - 19). The Jews in captivity were descendants of Abraham and in spite of their failings were the representatives of his God, so even in their down-trodden state they were precious in the eyes of the Lord, too precious to allow a Gentile dog to devour them. Even when the king of Egypt would have harmed Sarai, the wife of Abram, God intervened by plaguing the king and his household (Gen 12:14 - 20). At almost the end of the OT the prophet Zechariah wrote concerning the inhabitants of Zion, "he that toucheth you, toucheth the apple of his eye" (2:8). Perhaps even to this day those who ill-treat the Jews are judged by God, as Hitler and others proved.

If God has such an interest in the seed of Abraham, we

need not question His concern for His heavenly people of this dispensation. While in the world they are sure to meet with opposition and at times suffer wrongfully, those who take advantage of their weakness and meekness eventually come under His mighty hand. Herod slew James with the sword, but was soon eaten with worms. The infant church was scattered from Jerusalem, but in AD 70 the Romans scattered the inhabitants of the city to the ends of the earth. The principle expressed in the solemn words, "Whatsoever a man soweth, that shall he also reap" (Gal 6:7), has not been changed or nullified. Some might say, "What about Paul? Did he not persecute the saints?". Yes he did, and he was forgiven though he was the chief of sinners, but all have to agree that as God's ambassador he suffered the very evils which he had inflicted on others in his unsaved days. He cast saints into prison, and he was cast into one; he saw Stephen stoned, and was himself stoned; he put some to death, and he was executed.

A very important matter exemplified in this book is God's way with world empires. During the course of history certain nations have risen to supreme importance, and it is interesting to note how the knowledge of God was allowed to penetrate into the heart of even the vilest of these. Perhaps we are right in thinking that in the days of the patriarchs Egypt was the mistress of the world. We must notice that into that land the light of God's power was allowed to penetrate. Joseph's interpretation of the dreams convinced Pharaoh that a superior spirit dwelt in him. About two hundred and ten years later the same nation was visited by Moses, and again the power of Israel's God was demonstrated to them, not only in the plagues but in the destruction of their proud army in the Red Sea. The nations of Canaan were more of a combination of nations than a single domineering one, but again the power of the Almighty was brought to them in an unmistakable way. In David's time the Philistines had risen to great heights, but with his sling and stone, and later with his sword, he taught them that his God was supreme. When we reach the times of the Gentiles the same principle exists, for no sooner had Nebuchadnezzar begun to rule the great world empire than Daniel and his fellows were allowed to show him the wisdom of the true God. At the end of that kingdom Daniel was made the third ruler, and that because by divine help he could read the writing on the wall. The Persian empire followed with Daniel at the head of all the princes. This narrative brings us to almost the end of that mighty power where we see Mordecai as its prime minister, and, more important still, a Jewess as its queen. Just as "the spider takes hold with her hands, and is in kings' palaces", so God allows His witnesses to penetrate into high places, and bring the knowledge of Him to those who sit in darkness. When we enter the NT the dominant power is seen to be Rome. The chosen vessel to carry the news of God to the heart of that great empire was Paul. He stood alone in Rome, and at his defence preached the gospel to the Gentile world which was represented there. Can we doubt that even in our day the same principle operates, although we may not know the details of it?

Another subject that lies on the surface of this book is that of sowing and reaping. When dealing with this we mostly think of evil and its results, but this book shows us that good also yields a harvest. Mordecai sacrificed to rear Esther, and in a sense she owed her life to him. The day came when she was instrumental in saving his life. He also preserved Ahasuerus from an early grave, and later he himself was spared by the king. The harvest of his refusal to grant divine honours to a Gentile dog was reaped by him acquiring all that the proud man possessed. His faithfulness at the king's gate was rewarded by a seat next to the king. In doing what was right he was not thinking of its results, but time proved to him that it paid good dividends. May we "not be weary in well doing: for in due season we shall reap, if we faint not" (Gal 6:9).

Many of the women in Scripture are mentioned in association with failure, such as Eve, the first woman, and few of them whose histories are given are free from blame, even if it be of a minor nature. Esther the queen is an exception, for her story demonstrates that her conduct was not only without blame, but was marked by wisdom and honour. In the dark shades of a heathen palace she shines like a star in a black sky. Indeed most think that her name means "star", and if this be so, her conduct justified her appellation. There are special temptations for the faithful in high places. Quite a few who did well when the wind was in their faces, proved their weakness when exalted to positions of honour. Not all have a head for climbing, so some become dizzy when exalted to abnormal heights. Neither her beauty, nor her position as queen of the world's greatest empire at that time, in any way inflated her pride, nor did it divide her from her kindred, or her people. Samuel had to remind Saul of the change that had come about in his life, with the words, "When thou wast little in thine own sight... the Lord anointed thee king over Israel", but alas! he had become proud and rebellious, so the kingdom was taken from him (1 Sam 15:17). For a maid of humble birth, an orphan, and a member of a captive people, to find herself with a golden crown upon her head as queen of a great empire, and withal to remain humble and wise, is one of the wonders of this story.

A further trial in Esther's life, and one which must have proved hard to endure, was the loss of all her Jewish friends except her cousin. The captives in the lands of their adoption must have kept in close touch with one another, so that even the religion of their fathers could be kept alive in their hearts. In her childhood days she, like other Jewesses, would have felt at home with her kith and kin, but once called to the palace this suddenly came to an end. To be thrown into a den of heathendom, and to be surrounded with every evil device to gratify the lusts of corrupt nature, must have been no small shock to her, and a severe test to her personal convictions. Can we imagine the distracting thoughts which must have passed through her mind, and how often she must have asked herself, "Why has life for me turned out to be what it is?". It is easy for us with hindsight to understand that all was arranged by divine purpose, but all must have appeared to her as a profound mystery.

Stamped upon the pages of this book is another lesson about which those in normal life know little. It is that being head of a large empire is a dangerous post. History shows that the lives of kings are often seen as hanging on a thread. In spite of being surrounded by officers and body guards, they are constantly living in dread of the assassin. Even Ahasuerus was all but slain, and that by two of his trusted chamberlains, had not Mordecai discovered the plot and raised the alarm. Later he was assassinated by two of his officers, so in spite of every precaution, his life was taken from him. All are aware that if the king leads his army against the enemy in the battlefield he is in serious peril. What is surprising is that even in his own palace the eastern monarch was no less in danger. This consciousness of danger explains to us why it was so difficult to obtain an audience with the king. He had to be sure that all who approached him were his friends, and that no evil intent was in their visit. The extent of deceit in these high circles likewise amazes us. Haman could be the chief adviser to the king, and at all times was welcomed into his presence, yet at the same time he was plotting to exterminate the people of the queen, and indeed the queen herself, had the full intent of his plan been executed. Satan has been a liar and a deceiver from the beginning, and his character is manifested in his dupes.

An outstanding example of divine strategy is demonstrated in this book, but this can be discovered only when the entire story is read. What to the mind of the natural man appear to be mere matters of chance, can be seen by those who know God to be the working out of divine master plans. An orphan girl was granted the favour of good looks, was chosen out of a group of young maidens to be the queen instead of Vashti, was then in a position to plead for her people, and to be instrumental in preventing their destruction. Who but God could have so overruled and so planned the separate details, so that everything fitted together like a jigsaw puzzle? He not only works His sovereign will, but has the instruments prepared to act as required; and they do so at times without knowing what are His plans. More surprising to us is the fact that in all this grand programme His name is never mentioned, nor is He given any credit for its completion.

The suddenness of the changes which appear in this story is another fact worthy of consideration. Whether we think of the king having his banquet spoiled by the queen, or the queen being divorced, or of Haman's exaltation and fall, or of the grief of Mordecai at learning of the plot, or of his deliverance, all took place in a remarkably short space of time. "Boast not thyself of tomorrow; for thou knowest not what a day may bring forth" (Prov 27:1) is a text that is vividly illustrated in this book. There was nothing dull or monotonous around Shushan, for everything was constantly changing, so none felt secure in his position. Perhaps we too need to be reminded that we are in a changing world, and that earthly treasures or honours are of little value, for these can swiftly flee away. It is well that we who are the Lord's are promised a kingdom which cannot be moved, so we can forego the pleasures of this passing scene, and live in anticipation of that which is eternal.

A final lesson, and a serious one, is the importance of embracing opportunities. Some of these come only once in a lifetime, and if missed can cause deep regret. Esther had one such opportunity which she embraced with a trembling heart. It is all but impossible to truly estimate how much depended upon her intervention. In a sense it cost her her life, for she risked it for her people. We could compare her to David facing the giant with a sling and stones. Neither he nor she regretted facing the peril involved, for both acted for the good of their people. The Lord has His instruments on earth to fulfil His will, and He fits them for the times of their existence. It is folly to wish that we had been alive at a different time, or to imagine that we would have fitted better into a former or future age. Esther played her role with wisdom and skill, and it would have been foolish of her to wish she had been living at sometime other than when she was.

APPENDIX B

SUMMARY OF TYPICAL TEACHING IN ESTHER

Like most other historical books in the OT, the book of Esther contains several episodes which are shadows of things to come. To call these types may be an exaggeration, but to those who know future events they are most suggestive. In the course of our consideration of the book we have mentioned most of these as we went along, but by collecting them together they may be even more clear to our minds, and more impressed upon them.

The feasting at Shushan, coming as it does before the time of trouble for the Jews, reminds us of the short time of peace that will characterise the world after the rapture of the Church. It is obvious that during the first half of the prophetic week there will be much that will tempt the faithful to become worldly. With the covenant signed between the beast, the head of the revived Roman Empire, and the Jews, they will assume that all is well with them. The warning, "Take heed to yourselves, lest at any time your hearts be over charged with surfeiting, and drunkenness" (Luke 21:34) implies that such temptations will exist at that time. The happy times around Shushan were soon to end, and war with its sorrows was soon to follow. Even so the "peace and safety" of this world will be disturbed at the coming of the Lord as a thief in the night (1 Thess 5:2). The marriage of Esther to Ahasuerus is a suggestive reminder of the union of Jew and Gentile in that day, a union which will be ratified by the signing of the covenant for one week (Dan 9:27).

The sudden rise of Haman to power and influence is typical of the rise of the first beast of Rev 13. He too will demand the worship of all, but this will be refused by the faithful who will not wear his name and number. These faithful souls of the future are typified by Mordecai, who refused to bow in reverence before Haman. The plan devised by this wicked enemy to destroy the Jews, corresponds to the great united effort in the future, when all nations will be gathered around Jerusalem to destroy it, and those besieged in it. The sorrow of Mordecai and all the Jews is a vivid picture of "the time of Jacob's trouble" (Jer 30:7), when, as in the Book of Esther, the extermination of the nation will be attempted. Esther's intervention, even at the risk of losing her life, and her intercession which followed remind us of Christ's death and His present concern for His earthly people. All her actions and pleadings were done in the absence of the Jews, whose lives she sought to spare. Just as all hopes for their survival depended upon Esther, so all hope of deliverance for the remnant will depend upon the coming of Christ. The sudden destruction of the arch enemy and his sons, as the result of her pleading, is a foreshadowing of the destruction of the beast and all associated with him.

The decree of Haman brought to the surface the enemies of the Jews. Once it was circulated then all opposed to them throughout the empire were seen in their true colours. Likewise the tribulation period will be the test of the world, in that it will manifest those who are on the Lord's side. "Inasmuch as ye have done it unto one of the least of these my brethren, ye have done it unto me" (Matt 25:40). The numbers slain by the Jews are a picture of the judgment of the living nations, who at that time will be rewarded according to their attitude toward the faithful remnant.

The exaltation of Mordecai, his riding through the city, and his rising to lofty heights in administrative responsibility are suggestive of the part the nation of Israel will play in the future millennial kingdom. She has been at the tail of nations for a long time, but will eventually become their head.

The feast of Purim, in a faint way, is a foreshadowing of the coming time of prosperity and peace that the world will enjoy when Christ is reigning over it. Not until the Jews are restored to their rightful place will the earth be filled with the peace which men have striven so long to secure.

May our consideration of this book increase our confidence in God, and cause us to value not only His dealings with us, but also the great fact that He is working out His own purposes in the world, even though man may not acknowledge Him nor understand what He is doing.